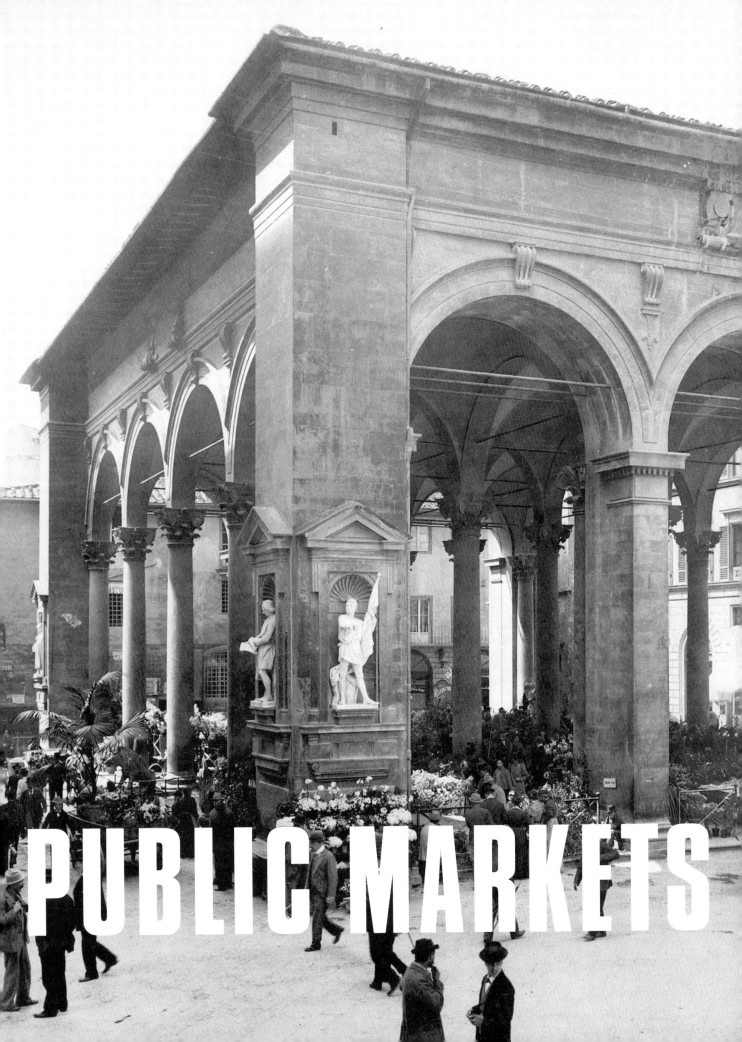

PUBLIC MARKETS

NORTON / LIBRARY OF CONGRESS

VISUAL SOURCEBOOKS IN ARCHITECTURE,

DESIGN, AND ENGINEERING

HELEN TANGIRES

W. W. Norton & Company, New York and London

In association with the Library of Congress

PUBLIC MARKETS

For information about permission to reproduce
selections from this book, write to Permissions,
W. W. Norton & Company, Inc., 500 Fifth Avenue,
New York, N.Y. 10110

Manufacturing by Quebecor World-Mexico
Book design by Kristina Kachele Design llc
Production Manager: Leeann Graham
Indexing by Bob Elwood

Library of Congress Cataloging-in-Publication Data

Tangires, Helen, 1956-
Public Markets/ Helen Tangires.
p. cm. – (Norton/Library of Congress
visual sourcebooks in architecture, design,
and engineering)
Includes bibliographical references and index.
ISBN: 978-0-393-73167-5 (hardcover)
1. Markets—United States. 2. Architecture—
United States. I. Title.

NA6273.T36 2007
725'.210973—dc22

2007001504

ISBN 13: 978-0-393-73167-5

W. W. Norton & Company, Inc.,
500 Fifth Avenue, New York, N.Y. 10110
www.wwnorton.com
W. W. Norton & Company Ltd., Castle House,
75/76 Wells St., London W1T 3QT

0 9 8 7 6 5 4 3 2 1

Center for Architecture, Design and Engineering
The Norton/Library of Congress Visual
Sourcebooks in Architecture, Design and
Engineering series is a project of the
Center for Architecture, Design and
Engineering in the Library of Congress,
established through a bequest from the
distinguished American architect Paul
Rudolph. The Center's mission is not only
to support the preservation of the
Library's enormously rich collections in
these subject areas, but also to increase
public knowledge of and access to them.
Paul Rudolph hoped that others would
join him in supporting these efforts. To
further this progress, and to support additional projects such as this one, the Library
of Congress is therefore pleased to accept
contributions to the Center for
Architecture, Design and Engineering
Fund or memorials in Mr. Rudolph's name
as additions to the Paul Rudolph Trust.

For further information on the Center
for American Architecture, Design and
Engineering, you may visit its website:
http://www.loc.gov/rr/print/adecen-
ter/adecent.html

C. FORD PEATROSS
CURATOR OF ARCHITECTURE,
DESIGN AND ENGINEERING

The Center for Architecture, Design and Engineering and the Publishing Office of the Library of Congress are pleased to join with W. W. Norton & Company to publish the pioneering series of the Norton/Library of Congress Visual Sourcebooks in Architecture, Design and Engineering.

Based on the unparalleled collections of the Library of Congress, this series of handsomely illustrated books draws from the collections of the nation's oldest federal cultural institution and the largest library in the world, with more than 130 million items on approximately 530 miles of bookshelves. The collections include more than 19 million books, 2.7 million recordings, 12 million photographs, 4.8 million maps, and 58 million manuscripts.

The subjects of architecture, design, and engineering are threaded throughout the rich fabric of this vast archive, and the books in this new series will serve not only to introduce researchers to the illustrations selected by their authors, but also to build pathways to adjacent and related materials, and even entire archives—to millions of photographs, drawings, prints, views, maps, rare publications, and written information in the general and special collections of the Library of Congress, much of it unavailable elsewhere.

Each volume serves as an entry to the collections, providing a treasury of select visual material, much of it in the public domain, for students, scholars, teachers, researchers, historians of art, architecture, design, technology, and practicing architects, engineers, and designers of all kinds.

A CD-ROM accompanying each volume contains high-quality, downloadable versions of all the illustrations. It offers a direct link to the Library's online, searchable catalogs and image files, including the hundreds of thousands of high-resolution photographs, measured drawings, and data files in the Historic American Buildings Survey, Historic American Engineering Record, and, eventually, the recently inaugurated Historic American Landscape Survey. The Library's Web site has rapidly become one of the most popular and valuable locations on the Internet, experiencing over three billion hits a year and serving audiences ranging from school children to the most advanced scholars throughout the world, with a potential usefulness that has only begun to be explored.

Among the subjects to be covered in this series are building types, building materials and details; historical periods and movements; landscape architecture and garden design; interior and ornamental design and furnishings; and industrial design. *Public Markets* is an excellent exemplar of the goals and possibilities on which its series is based.

JAMES H. BILLINGTON
THE LIBRARIAN OF CONGRESS

The introduction to this book provides a general history of public buildings and spaces devoted to the marketplace for fresh food. As the rich resources of the Library of Congress attest, public markets persist as the most enduring and universal form of urban food marketing and distribution worldwide. The balance of the book is divided into sections that focus on specific market types, beginning with the most basic open-air marketplaces and ending with the more architecturally complex wholesale markets. The final section illustrates the people and activities associated with market day. Figure-number prefixes designate the section.

Short captions give the essential identifying information: subject, location, date, creator(s) of the image, and the Library of Congress call number, which can be used to find the image online. Note that a link to the Library of Congress Web site may be found on the CD.

AM	American Memory
ADE	Architecture, Design, and Engineering Drawings
AFC	American Folklife Center
AHC	Archive of Hispanic Culture
Brum	William C. Brumfield Photograph Collection
DETR (formerly DPCC)	Detroit Publishing Company Collection
FSA/OWI	Farm Security Administration/Office of War Information Collection
G&M	Geography and Map Division
Genthe	Arnold Genthe Collection: Negatives and Transparencies
GSC	Gottscho–Schleisner Collection
HABS	Historic American Building Survey
Hory	Theodor Horydczak Collection
LC	Library of Congress
LOOK	Look Magazine Collection
MPBRS	Motion Picture, Broadcasting, and Recorded Sound Division
MRC	Microform Reading Room
NCLC	National Child Labor Committee
NYWTS	New York World Telegram & Sun Newspaper Photograph Collection
P&P	Prints and Photographs Division
PCHROM	Photochrom Prints Collection
PGA	Popular Graphic Arts
Postcards	Postcards of American Scenery and Subjects, Sorted by State Name
Prok	Prokudin—Gorskii Collection
RBSCD	Rare Book and Special Collection Division
SSF	Subject Specfic File
USN&WR	U.S. News & World Report Magazine Collection
WTCPC	World's Transportation Commission Photograph Collection

CONTENTS

THE PUBLIC MARKET TRADITION

IN-002

IN-003

The activity of buying and selling food has shaped our cities and towns for centuries, since an urban population by nature depends on others for agricultural production. At the heart of this activity stands the public market—the buildings and spaces in which vegetables, meat, produce, and other commodities intended for human consumption are sold by diverse persons from numerous spaces or stalls, all under a common authority. Although a public market need not necessarily be located on public land or owned by a public entity, it has public goals and creates a public space—features that distinguish it from a roadside stand, grocery store, supermarket, or other independently owned food retailing establishment.[1] It also has the unique status of being the most enduring, universal form of urban food marketing and distribution—with roots as old as cities themselves.[2]

DEFINING THE BOUNDARIES OF EXCHANGE

Markets first appeared in history as specifically appointed places of exchange, usually bounded by lakes, rivers, forests, or boundary stones. Such meeting places were neutral territory, or thresholds of exchange, where differing groups gathered peacefully for their mutual benefit. Pillars, posts, crosses, and other landmarks designated these sanctioned places (IN-003).[3]

In antiquity, the official marketplace was located in the civic center—a large open square reserved for all public functions. The civic center, or *agora* as it was known in the ancient Greek world, served as the site not only for trade and commerce but also for administrative, legislative, judicial, social, and religious activities. The location of markets in the agora was convenient for city dwellers, vendors bringing goods by road or water, and officials

9

IN-004

responsible for overseeing the markets. Vendors sold from temporary wooden booths in the open air marketplace or from rented shops in covered colonnades known as *stoas*.[4] The *forum*, counterpart to the agora in imperial Rome, likewise served as the principal place of commerce. The marketplaces of antiquity are the predecessors of the great piazzas and squares in Europe, and some have been in continuous use, such as the Piazza Erbe in Verona, Italy, located on the site of the Roman forum (IN-004–IN-006).[5]

In addition to civic centers, streets also provided practical locations for markets since they were already publicly owned and they provided natural boundaries. Usually the street of choice was not only wide enough for both a market and a thoroughfare, but also oriented along a prominent north-south or east-west axis of a grid plan for the convenience of farmers and tradesmen bringing their goods. Some cities allocated different streets to different markets in order to rationalize trade by type of commodity; and they distributed multiple markets geographically, usually by ward or neighborhood, so that the markets did not compete with each other (IN-007–IN-010).[6]

The designation of particular streets and squares for market purposes fostered the development of entire commercial districts. Markets in the Islamic world, known as *bazaars* or *souks*, were and still are cities in themselves, encompassing sometimes hundreds of shops and covered streets housing commercial trades and crafts, in addition to warehouses, inns, eating establishments, public baths, and other institutions that support the market (IN-011–IN-013).[7]

IN-005

IN-006

IN-004. Gate of Athena Archegetis, the western propylon of the Roman agora, Athens, Greece. Neue Photographische Gesellschaft A.G., Berlin-Steglitz, 1905. P&P,LC-USZ62-116561.

During the Roman period, the Athenians built a new market just east of the main agora and dedicated it to Caesar and Augustus around AD 100. It contained a large rectangular colonnade of shops around an open court and was approached by this monumental Doric propylon, or gate.

IN-005. View of the forum, Rome, Italy. DETR, ca. 1890–1900. P&P,LC-DIG-ppmsc-06605(color).

IN-006. Piazza delle Erbe, Verona, Italy. P&P,Foreign Geog File, Italy, Verona. LC-DIG-ppmsca-12310.

The rectangular Roman forum from the city's original layout formed the basis for the piazza.

This page
IN-007. New Orleans, Showing Location of Markets. ca. 1908. G&M,City Maps-New Orleans-Marketing,19—?.

At the time of this map, New Orleans had more public markets than any other city in the United States.

IN-008. A Plan of Charles-ton in Cecil County, Maryland. G&M,G3844.C34G46 17—.P55.

IN-009. Leadenhall Market, London. From Ogilby & Morgan, *Large and Accurate Map of the City of London* (1677). Facsimile, London & Middlesex Archaeological Society, 1895. G&M,London,England,1677, detail.

IN-010. Map of the city of Cincinnati, from actual survey by Joseph Gest, city surveyor, 1838. Wm. Haviland, engraver. G&M,G4084.C4 1838 .G4, detail.

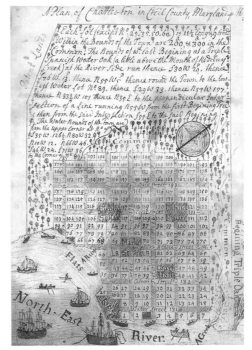

IN-008

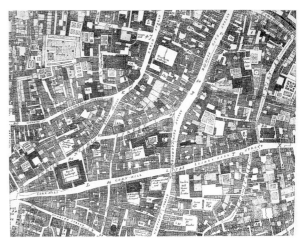

IN-009

IN-007

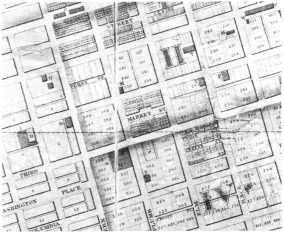

IN-010

IN-011

IN-012

IN-013

IN-014

REGULATING THE MARKETPLACE

Over the centuries a host of edicts, laws, ordinances, and religious codes—grouped here under the general term "market laws"—has guided the ethics of trade in fresh food. Market laws established guidelines for all types of activities, ranging from when and where fish may be sold and how animals could be slaughtered, to the pricing of goods and the use of standard weights and measures. Local authorities developed rules and regulations that attracted food producers into the city to ensure an adequate supply of fresh food at fair prices for the urban populace. Regulated public markets were critical to the survival of the town, because without them, unbridled competition and unfair dealings could jeopardize the public welfare.[8]

The most consistent market laws over time and place were those that restricted forestalling, or buying products before they reached the market—literally, before they reached the stall. Practical reasons dictated that food could not be sold beyond the legal boundaries of the public market. Consumers could enjoy the convenience of procuring everyday provisions from a single location and could choose among several vendors; the consolidation of market activities enabled the authorities to enforce health and sanitation codes, police the market, and collect revenues. Cities also were motivated to restrict sales to within the legal limits of the marketplace in order to guarantee free and equal access to the food supply at a fair price (IN-015).

Although laws against forestalling dealt with people who purchased goods outside of the formal bounds of the market, legislation was also necessary to prevent vendors from buying goods inside the market for resale. Known as regrating, from the Old French *regra-*

teor, meaning peddler or huckster, this practice was forbidden or closely circumscribed, in order to encourage people to buy directly from the producer and to promote centralized competition.

Market laws also reflected a concern for protecting the trades with strict allocation of vocational duties and opportunities. Only a licensed butcher in an official stall or in an official place of standing could cut up meat in quarters, joints, or small pieces in the public markets (IN-016). Violators, known as shiners, shirkers, or sharks, were either vendors posing as country butchers, butchers who had lost their licenses but who continued to practice the trade illegally, or agents who sold on commission for farmers. Laws against shiners were intended to protect legitimate butchers from those who practiced the craft without paying the required fees for stall rent and licenses.

Although ordinances concerning weights and measures varied slightly from city to city, their principles were the same. They were intended to demonstrate government's duty and obligation to protect the public from profiteering, fraud, and cheating (IN-017). Market clerks inspected food for standard weight and measure, assigned stalls, collected rents and fines, and policed and swept the market. Food inspection was another responsibility of the clerks. Wholesome food was critical to the health and well-being of the community, and failure to enforce inspection laws could create a public health hazard, not to mention humiliation for local officials (IN-018).

Market authorities were also responsible for enforcing the "market peace"—a term that describes a protected environment in which buyers and sellers may carry on trade effectively. Maintaining the market peace included such acts as providing good roads to and from the market (IN-019–IN-020), protecting against thieves, and keeping the marketplace in good order. The enforcement of fixed market days and hours ensured that vendors had an equal opportunity to conduct sales. Likewise, the traditional practice known as the market cycle, in which markets in proximity to one another were open on different days, kept multiple markets from interfering with each other. In short, enforcing the peace involved providing a safe and attractive environment for buyers and sellers, in both the physical and the economic sense.

RULES
REGULATING THE MARKET!

Provost Marshal's Office,
Beaufort, N.C., July 28, 1864.

All fresh provisions will be sold on Market Wharf. Market boats are not permitted to land at any other wharf, and persons arriving in said boats will report in person at this office. The intention is to accommodate ALL PERSONS, and to this end sales will be limited. No special permits will be given to any officer, soldier, or citizen, to purchase extra supplies, and sales at the wharf for purpose of speculation are forbidden. The limitation of purchases will be regulated by the Guard, under special orders from this office.

The following are the MAXIMUM prices to be asked for the articles enumerated below, and the Guard will arrest any person violating, or attempting to violate, these regulations:

MEATS.

Fresh Beef,	per lb.,	$0 18
" Pork,	"	16
" Mutton,	"	18
" Veal,	"	18
Ham,	"	30
Venison,	"	25

POULTRY, &c.

Turkeys,	each	1 25
Geese,	"	1 00
Ducks, (tame)	"	50
" (Canvass back)	"	50
" Other varieties,	per pair,	1 00
Chickens, (large)		90
" (middling)		60
Pigeons,	per dozen,	1 00
Quails, (or Partridges)	"	1 00
Eggs,	"	30

FISH.

Shad,	per lb.,	10
Other fish, from 5c. to 7c. per lb., according to quality.		
Salt Fish,	per lb.,	08
Oysters, (large)	per gallon or bushel,	60
" (middling)	"	45
Clams,	"	50
Crabs, (soft)	per dozen,	40
" (stone)	"	85
Terrapins,	each,	15

VEGETABLES.

Potatoes, (sweet)	per bushel,	1 00
" (Irish)	"	1 50
Beans (string)	per peck,	30
Tomatoes,	"	25
Peas,	"	40
Beets,	"	25
Turnips,	"	25
Onions,	"	30
Corn,	per dozen ears,	25
Cucumbers,	per dozen,	20
Cabbage,	head,	10

FRUITS.

Peaches,	per peck,	1 00
Pears,	"	75
Apples,	"	50
Plums,	per quart,	10
Currants,	"	20
Grapes,	per peck,	50
Berries,	per quart,	15
Watermelons,	each,	30
Muskmelons,	"	20

MISCELLANEOUS.

Honey,	per lb.	25
Beeswax,	"	60
Otter Skins,		2 00 to 4 00

WALTER S. POOR,
Lt. Col. & Provost Marshal,
Beaufort, N.C.

IN-015

IN-016

IN-017

IN-015. "Rules Regulating the Market," Beaufort, North Carolina. Broadside, July 28, 1864. P&P,Portfolio 135,Folder 15.

IN-016. Frontispiece. From James Plumtre, *The Experienced Butcher* (1816). Gen. Coll.,TS1960.P6. LC-DIG-ppmsca-12671.

IN-017. FSA county supervisor McArthur weighs in chickens for market, Coffee County, Alabama. John Collier, photographer, 1941. P&P,FSA/OWI,LC-USF34-080425-D.

IN-018

IN-019

IN-020

IN-018. "Our exposure of the swill milk trade." From *Frank Leslie's Illustrated Newspaper* 5 (May 22, 1858): 385. P&P,LC-USZ62-121642,detail. Health warden Frank Leslie and his corps witness the dissection of a cow at the Offal Dock, foot of Forty-Fifth Street, East River, New York City.

IN-019. Farmers coming to market at Seoul through the Peking Pass, the highway to Manchuria and China, Korea. Underwood & Underwood, 1904. P&P,LC-USZ62-72547.

IN-020. The old French Market, New Orleans, Louisiana. William Henry Jackson, photographer, ca. 1880–1897. P&P,DETR,LC-D418-8113.

IN-021

IN-021. Vegetable market, Cavite, Philippine Islands, Kingsley-Barnes & Neuner Company, ca. 1899. P&P,LC-USZ62-112471.

opposite
IN-022. Market, Chefang, China, 1939 or 1940. P&P,FSA/OWI,LC-USW33-043084-ZC.

IN-023. Alphabet [A—M] illustrated with scenes of street cries. From *The Uncle's Present . . .* (n.d.). RBSCD,PE110.A1U5,P&P,LC-USZ62-55353,detail.

IN-024. Poultry peddler in Greek costume, Athens, Greece. B. L. Singley (Keystone View Company), photographer, 1895. P&P,LC-USZ62-65904.

Public markets in all parts of the world are still regulated to a degree by national, state, or local authorities, as well as by tradition. Officials issue permits and licenses, inspect goods, oversee weights and measures, collect market revenues, ensure that vendors honor posted market days and hours, and enforce all other rules of the market.

MARKET TYPOLOGIES

The desire to maintain an orderly trading environment and offer protection from the elements has led to a variety of market types through the ages.[9] The most ubiquitous and consistent type is the open-air marketplace. Usually devoid of permanent structures, it is defined physically by the boundaries of a public square, and in temporal terms by specific market days and hours. Shelter may come from trees or from awnings, umbrellas, and other temporary fixtures provided by vendors (IN-021–IN-022). Street markets share similar kinds of boundaries and definitions with the open air marketplace, although they tend to assume a more linear form. Beyond the boundaries of the marketplace are street vendors (IN-023–IN-024), whose ambulatory privileges permit them to sell staples and ready-made foods in restricted places. These markets on the move have developed their own type of "structures" necessitated by their mobility and the absence of permanent facilities.

Public markets may also operate on an open, ground floor of a public building such as a courthouse or town hall. This form has its origins in medieval Europe, where a combined town hall and market was designed for trading on an open, arcaded ground floor, above which stood one or more stories for administration of the local government. In this type

IN-022

IN-023

IN-024

of structure, marketing is secondary to the main purpose of the building (IN-025–IN-026).

The freestanding shed is the most common type of market structure, and one that lends itself well to location in a street or square (IN-027). The shed has been a standard market type throughout the world since antiquity. Open or partially closed, it consists of arches, columns, or piers supporting a low pitched gable roof, sometimes with projecting eaves to increase the amount of covered trading space (IN-028). Sheds provide minimal protection from the elements for the least cost and can be erected quickly relative to more substantial structures. Sometimes they are built as a string of separate structures that allow for cross traffic and for separating the sale of food types, as in Philadelphia and Charleston (see 5-021 and 5-027); or they might take the form of colonnades arranged in a square around an open court—a style with antique origins and one that is still popular in the Hispanic world (IN-030).

In part, the shed owes its popularity to the fact that builders are familiar with construction techniques that employ a modular bay system for similar structures such as barns and churches, in order to achieve the desired enclosure (see 5-001). In addition, the multiple entrances make the facility attractive and accessible to patrons coming from any direction; the shed's openness facilitates air circulation and the unloading of goods; and it is easy to wash down at the end of the market day (IN-029).

The enclosed market house was the type of choice in the late eighteenth and early nineteenth centuries. Coinciding with the imperative to improve the flow of traffic and to modernize urban space was a drive to eliminate the apparent chaos and disorder of the open air

IN-025. Market hall, Ross-on-Wye, England. Unidentified photographer, ca. 1890–1910. P&P,PCHROM,LC-DIG-ppmsc-08819(color).

This market house was built of local red sandstone around 1660. It consists of a ground floor arcade and a single chamber on the second story. The clock tower may be a nineteenth-century addition. The building is used today as a cultural heritage center.

IN-026. Southern Market and Municipal Building, Mobile, Alabama. Unidentified photographer, ca. 1906. P&P,DETR,LC-D4-19451.

Thomas Simmons James designed the market in 1855. It is brick covered with white-washed stucco and has wrought-iron detailing. The cupola is made of cypress wood. Meat and vegetable vendors occupied stalls on the ground floor of the central section, and the wing at right was the fish market. By 1857 the second floor over the fish market contained a drill room and armory for the First Volunteer Regiment. The remaining sections of the building were for municipal offices.

IN-027

IN-028

IN-027. Catharine Market, around 1850, New York. Samuel Hollyer, engraver, 1903. P&P,LC-USZ62-93760.

IN-028. The old French Market, New Orleans, Louisiana. William Henry Jackson, photographer, ca. 1880–1897. P&P,DETR,LC-D418-8114.

IN-029. Typical municipal market, Philippine Islands. From *Architectural Record* 41, no. 5 (1917). Gen. Coll.,NA1.A6. LC-DIG-ppmsca-12687.

IN-030. Market in Aguascalientes, Mexico. William Henry Jackson, photographer, 1891. P&P,DETR,LC-D43-T01-1120.

IN-029

IN-030

IN-031

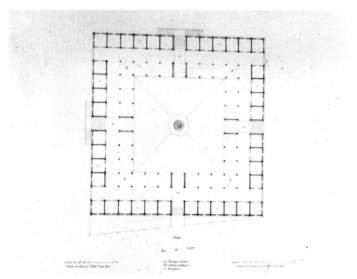

IN-032

market. Architects in nineteenth-century France were active in designing new buildings to rationalize and contain marketing. The market in Nevers (IN-031–IN-032) typifies the enclosed market house popular in France in the early nineteenth century—a series of rectangular wood or masonry structures with clerestories, arranged in a square around an open court with a fountain in the center.

British architects also looked for new strategies to contain markets physically, while encouraging the supply and demand for fresh food. The London-based architect Charles Fowler (1792–1867), for example, transformed the former open air market at Covent Garden into a fashionable complex of arcades and shops. The new Covent Garden Market, designed in 1828–1830, had become London's principal market for fruits and vegetables. Fowler created a unified complex of three parallel buildings surrounded by arcades, connected by corner lodges for eating houses and specialty shops. Horses and carts occupied the open space between the buildings (IN-033–IN-034).[10]

IN-033. Covent Garden, circa 1720.
Engraving by Sutton Nicholls. From
Architectural Review 41, no. 245 (April
1917): plate 1. Gen. Coll.,NA1.A69. LC-DIG-
ppmsca-12670.

IN-034. Bird's-eye view of Covent Garden,
London, England. From *Architectural Review*
41, no. 246 (April 1917): 99. Gen.
Coll.,NA1.A69. LC-DIG-ppmsca-12669.

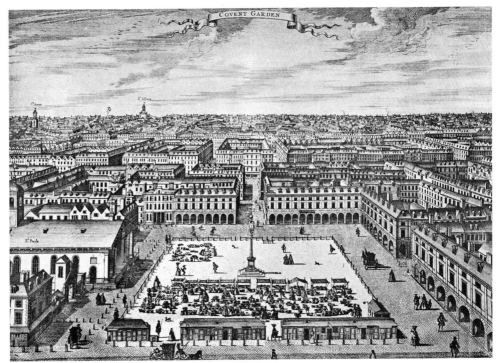

IN-033

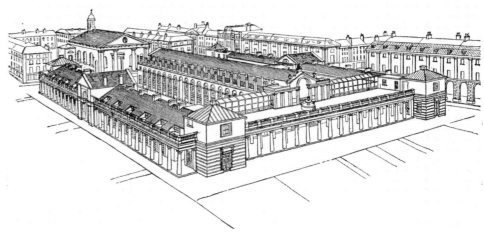

IN-034

Developments in iron and glass construction continued to foster the preference for
enclosed market houses. The French state, in support of its iron industry, encouraged
architects to consider ways to incorporate iron into their structures. Architects responded
initially by using iron for wall ties, roofs, floors, and interior columns. The most daring
use of iron for construction began with Les Halles, the principal market in Paris, designed
by Victor Baltard (1805–1874) and Felix-Emmanuel Callet (1791–1854) (IN-036; see 7-001–
7-007). Baltard and Callet conceived of the market as a series of modular pavilions with
exposed cast-iron exterior and interior supports. The functional, aesthetic, and economical qualities of iron and glass markets inspired generations of architects and engineers to
improve on the design. One aim was the development of roof truss systems to provide the
desired height for light and air, without the need for interior supports, since unobstruct-
ed floor space was highly desirable in markets (IN-035).[11]

IN-035

IN-036

IN-035. Marché de l'Ave Maria, Paris, France. From *La Construction Moderne*, February 6, 1886, plate 31. Gen. Coll.,NA2.C7. LC-DIG-ppmsca-12647.

IN-036. Les Halles, Paris, France. Michael Vaccaro, photographer, 1955. P&P,LOOK Job55-3887-F,frame 24. LC-DIG-ppmsca-12336.

Interior columns supported the walls of the clerestory.

Architects and engineers in England also manufactured cast-iron parts for prefabricated market houses, not only for domestic use but also for export to the English colonies. By the end of the century the young nations of Latin America, including Mexico, Brazil, and Argentina, also embraced the prefabricated iron market house as a means of imposing order to the streets and as a statement of modernity.[12]

Markets that combine the wholesale and retail trade—referred to as central markets in the second half of the nineteenth century—were clearing places for food from neighboring and distant regions and forwarding centers for other retail outlets. Central markets were designed to accommodate under one roof the retailer (one who buys goods in large quantities from the producer either directly or through a wholesaler, and then sells individual items or small quantities to the customer) and the wholesaler (one who sells in bulk for the convenience of grocers, hucksters, hotels, restaurants, and other purchasers who buy in large quantities).

Although historically wholesalers were not permitted or were severely restricted in the public markets, large cities found it convenient to tolerate, and thus accommodate, them in their principal marketplaces. Thus, some central markets were built originally for the retail trade and then evolved into central markets as the wholesale trade developed. For example, Faneuil Hall Market in Boston served a population of 58,277, the majority of whom resided within one mile, when its cornerstone was laid in 1825. By 1870 Boston's population had grown to 648,525, and the majority of the trade was wholesale (IN-037).[13]

In the late nineteenth century, the European nations shared an interest in building cen-

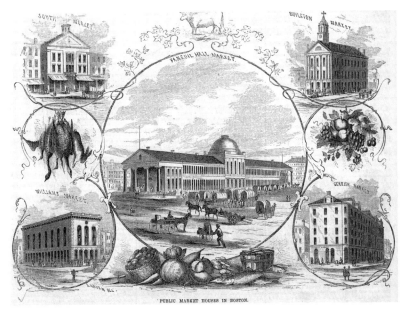

IN-037

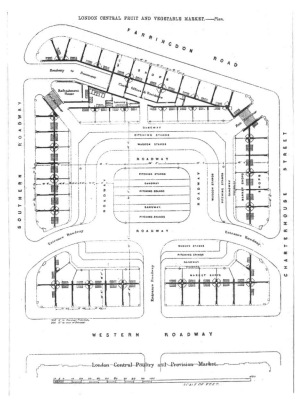

IN-039

IN-038

IN-037. "Public Market Houses in Boston," Massachusetts. From *Ballou's Pictorial Drawing-Room Companion*, August 15, 1855. P&P,AP2 .B227 (Casey). LC-DIG-ppmsca-12640.

Fanueil Hall Market, the centerpiece of Boston's public market system, is surrounded by vignettes of South, Boylston, Williams, and Gerrish markets.

IN-038. London Central Fruit and Vegetable Market. From *Builder* 38 (1880): 71–72. Gen. Coll.,NA1.B5. LC-DIG-ppmsca-12668.

IN-039. Plan, London Central Fruit and Vegetable Market. From *Builder* 38 (1880): 73. Gen. Coll.,NA1.B5. LC-DIG-ppmsca-12667.

tral markets to unify wholesalers under careful municipal administration and regulation. England was exemplary in its effort to integrate central markets with rail service, in order to regulate the wholesale trade on a regional and national level. Smithfield Market, London's principal market for meat, was serviced by three railways: the London, Chatham, and Dover; the Great Northern; and the Metropolitan. Designed by city architect Horace Jones, Smithfield had an underground freight terminal with loading docks from which meat was hoisted to the shops above. Jones also designed the mammoth London Central Fruit and Vegetable Market, noted for its solid construction, ventilation, distinct facilities for the wholesale and retail trades, off-street parking for wagons, and the separation of vehicular and pedestrian traffic (IN-038–IN-039).[14]

Berlin, shortly after becoming the capital of the German Empire in 1871, rationalized its food distribution system by building a series of uniform market houses distributed throughout the city. Simultaneous with their construction were new market laws that limited the type of sales to retail only. The city moved all wholesaling, formerly conducted in the open squares, to a new central market in Alexanderplatz. The Zentralmarkthalle, built according to plans by Hermann Wilhelm Albert Blankenstein (1829–1910), opened in 1886 and served as a hub for the city's food distribution system until it was destroyed in World War II.[15]

In the early decades of the twentieth century federal, state, and local governments throughout the world, from Tokyo to Buenos Aires, collaborated in the design and construction of new buildings and spaces for large-scale storage and regional distribution of food. Known as wholesale terminal markets, these markets unify the arrival of food by rail, water, and roads. They also facilitate the distribution of food away from the market—namely, to the various retail outlets throughout the city and region.[16]

The distinction between a central market and a wholesale terminal market is subtle. In general, the term "central market" fell out of use by the twentieth century, when cities preferred to locate their principal wholesale markets away from the center city. Furthermore, the wholesale terminal market (also called a produce terminal) might include auction houses, refrigerated warehouses, and other facilities not common to the central markets built in the nineteenth century. The wholesale terminal market, usually located in the semi-industrial section of a city, might also require its own bank or barber shop—institutions that central markets did not need to provide.

The wholesale terminal market is a complex whose principal buildings are the long and narrow rows of stores built of reinforced concrete, with front and back platforms for transferring loads. Other structures on the site may include an administration building for housing market officials, restaurants, retail stores, and other business activities catering to the public. The site might also include a produce shed, packing plant, auction house, cold storage plant, slaughterhouse, or cannery.

THE HISTORY OF PUBLIC MARKETS IN THE UNITED STATES

All of these market types—the open air marketplace, the street market, the street vendor, the market on the ground floor of a public building, the market shed, the enclosed market house, the central market, and the wholesale terminal market—have been part of the urban history of the United States. In addition to wharves, docks, bridges, and roads, cities and towns in the new nation were expected to provide facilities for the buying and selling of food. More than a mere convenience, it was the duty of the state to ensure the urban populace an adequate, wholesome, and affordable supply of necessities. Although licenses, price controls, and regulations were not limited to food vendors, the marketing of daily provisions under the careful guidance of the municipality was the overarching symbol of government's commitment to a well-ordered public economy. Deeply rooted in English and continental European common law, customs, and practices, the market laws, building typologies, and administrative practices in the United States mirrored those of their European antecedents.

The public market in nineteenth-century America was the primary source of the city's daily supply of fresh food. Local government made an effort to ensure its success not only by imposing regulations but also by carefully considering site, financing, public support, simplicity and flexibility in design, and a location convenient to buyers and sellers. These calculations were intended to reduce risk and speculation, important factors in the construction of other public buildings like the courthouse or city hall.[17]

Most remarkable has been the survival of public markets in the United States throughout the twentieth and into the twenty-first century, given the proliferation of alternative, private forms of urban food marketing and distribution, such as private markets (IN-040, IN-043) and grocery stores.[18] Furthermore, since the public market tradition gives priority to bringing the producer and consumer face to face, the system was all the more threatened by industrial forms of food production. As the Chicago meatpacking firms of Armour and Swift perfected the disassembly line, local butchers, traditionally the lifeblood of the public markets, lost their local supply of animals on the hoof. Thus, market butch-

IN-040

IN-041

ers either were driven out of business or were forced to become dealers of dressed meat (IN-041).[19]

Despite the odds, municipal reformers at the beginning of the twentieth century believed that well-run public markets could alleviate the urban evils of rising food costs, lack of fresh food, traffic congestion, and poor public hygiene. Local officials also believed that modern, attractive markets would improve the city's national and international image. This notion was part of the larger City Beautiful movement, whose promoters hoped that physical improvements would inculcate in citizens moral values and civic pride. The movement gave impetus to new market construction, such as the West Side Market in Cleveland. Private developers of new suburbs such as Lake Forest, Illinois, also incorporated markets into their planning, often with visual references to the historical markets of Europe (IN-042).

Also placing improved markets on its agenda was the Office of Markets of the United States Department of Agriculture (USDA), established in 1913 and elevated to Bureau status in 1917. The Bureau of Markets developed a model market system for cities across the nation—one that proposed three market types based on a city's size and local conditions. A curb market was recommended for cities whose population did not justify the cost of a permanent market building. This type of market was simply a designated place along a street curb or on a vacant lot where market wagons and trucks belonging to farmers and hucksters could be accommodated. A market house was the second type, recommended for cities that had an already-established public market in need of new facilities. Bureau architects provided model market plans on demand—plans that promoted durability and sanitation through the use of materials such as concrete, steel, glass, marble, brick, and

IN-040. Sheriff Street Market, Cleveland, Ohio. Unidentified photographer, 1905. P&P,DETR,LC-D4-18636.

Construction was financed by a market and cold storage company and was completed in 1891. Designed by Lehman and Schmitt, architects, the market was 400 feet long and consisted of two six-story buildings flanking a central domed pavilion. The side veranda at street level sheltered produce stalls. Inside, the market was divided into five aisles and contained 312 stands. Most of the structure was destroyed by fire in 1930.

IN-041. Dressing the beeves, Armour's great packing house, Chicago, U.S.A. Strohmeyer & Wyman, publishers, 1892. P&P,LC-USZ62-111763.

IN-042. Market Square, Lake Forest, Illinois. Howard Shaw, architect. From *Western Architect* 26 (October 1917): plate 13. Gen. Coll.,NA1.W4. LC-DIG-ppmsca-12662.

According to *Western Architect*, the new market square project was inspired by the old towns of Flanders and northern Germany.

IN-043. Interior of a Piggly Wiggly self-service grocery store in or near Memphis, Tennessee, with two turnstiles in foreground. Clifford H. Poland, photographer, 1918. P&P,LC-USZ62-91202.

The USDA also studied developments in private markets, such as the self-service grocery store. Its investigators, however, lamented the impersonality of the new system, particularly the turnstile, and the noticeable absence of human activity that had characterized life around the public markets.

IN-043

IN-042

IN-044

IN-044. West Side Market, Cleveland, Ohio. Hubbell and Benes, architects. From *U.S. Bureau of the Census, Municipal Markets in Cities Having a Population of over 30,000* (1919). Gen. Coll.,HF5472.U6 A5. LC-DIG-ppmsca-12666.

IN-045

IN-046

glazed tile (IN-044). For cities with a population over 100,000, the USDA recommended investment in wholesale terminal markets to facilitate food marketing and distribution on a large scale.[20]

State and local governments, assisted by the USDA, expanded their involvement in public food marketing, storage, and distribution. New York—the nation's largest metropolis and market for fresh food—fed a resident population of five million people as well as thousands of daily commuters; it also provisioned outgoing trains and transatlantic steamships, and it exported food to other cities and towns. The city established a Department of Markets in 1917. Whereas markets had previously fallen under the control of seven different municipal departments, the new Department of Markets had complete jurisdiction over and management of all public markets and marketplaces owned by the city. It consolidated power and authorized the market commissioner, among other things, to establish wholesale terminal markets and cold storage plants, beginning with a model wholesale terminal market in the Bronx (see 8-026–8-031).[21]

A new interest in wholesale markets, not only in New York but in other large cities across the country, was a direct response to the rise in large-scale agriculture and corporate control of food processing and distribution. These factors led government officials to worry that the food supply was falling out of public control (IN-045–IN-046).[22]

IN-047

IN-045. Large-scale agricultural gang labor. Dorothea Lange, photographer, 1939. P&P,FSA/OWI,LC-USF34-019234-C.

Caption reads: "Mexicans and whites from the Southwest pull, clean, tie and crate carrots for the eastern market for eleven cents per crate of forty-eight bunches. Many can make barely one dollar a day. Heavy oversupply of labor and competition for jobs is keen. Near Meloland, Imperial Valley." [California.]

IN-046. Loading fat lambs on narrow gauge railway for shipment to Denver market, Cimarron, Colorado. Russell Lee, photographer, 1940. P&P,FSA/OWI,LC-USF346-037468-D.

IN-047. Thirteenth Avenue Retail Market, Brooklyn, New York, New York. Phyllis Twachtman, photographer, 1965. P&P,NYWTS,Subj/Geog File-Markets-Thirteenth Avenue Market. LC-DIG-ppmsca-12772.

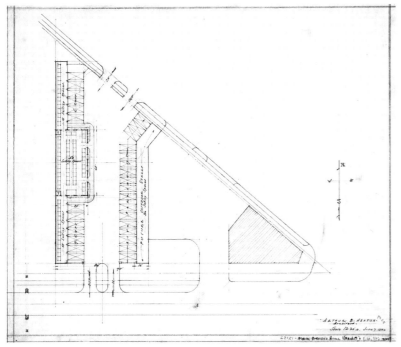

IN-048

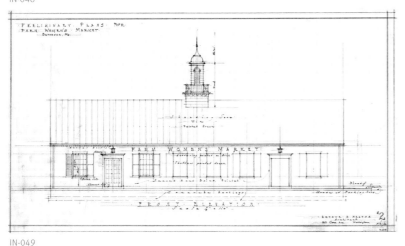

IN-049

IN-048. Selling spaces and future outdoor stalls, Farm Women's Market, Bethesda, Maryland. Arthur B. Heaton, architect, 1932. P&P,ADE-UNIT 648,no.3(C size). LC-DIG-ppmsca-12152.

IN-049. Preliminary plans for Farm Women's Market, Bethesda, Maryland. Arthur B. Heaton, architect, 1932. P&P,ADE-UNIT 648,no.6(C size). LC-DIG-ppmsca-12153.

Farm women's markets were established in the 1930s in an effort to promote the direct sale of local produce during the Depression. Fruits, vegetables, dairy products, poultry, and eggs are the most common items handled. Cooked foods, handicrafts, flowers, and nursery stock are also common. This market is still in operation.

During the New Deal, public markets were vital to government efforts to reduce agricultural surplus in the countryside and high food prices in the cities. Under the direction of Fiorello La Guardia, New York's mayor from 1934 to 1945, municipal architects working in the Department of Markets developed a series of enclosed market houses to replace several pushcart markets (IN-047). These market houses were fairly uniform in appearance and readily identifiable by their bold geometric form, broad horizontal bands of glazed and concrete surfaces, absence of sidewalk obstructions, and clear signage that was unambiguous in crediting the city. La Guardia was a major advocate of public markets and used his close ties to President Franklin Roosevelt to secure New Deal support for market construction and revitalization (see 9-015).

The Public Works Administration funded new market construction in cities such as Nashville, New Orleans, Shreveport, and Austin.[23] Government support for improved food marketing and distribution facilities also extended into rural communities, where cooperative markets and farm women's markets promoted the direct sale of local produce (IN-048–IN-049). Fruits, vegetables, dairy products, poultry, and eggs were the most common items handled. Cooked foods, handicrafts, flowers, and nursery stock were also for sale. These markets had minimal con-

IN-050

IN-051

IN-052

struction costs, since they employed the simple, open-air or partially enclosed market shed.

During the 1950s and 1960s, construction of new market houses waned in the United States, owing to several national trends in the postwar era. Public investment in new market construction declined with the rise of chain supermarkets (IN-050). Vendors in the public markets could not compete with the supermarket's economies of scale and capital investment, and many were forced out of business.[24] Corporate control of food processing and agribusiness also contributed to a decline in direct marketing, as did the development of the interstate highway system, which enabled the trucking industry to dominate the country's food distribution system.[25] These factors, coupled with urban renewal projects that often disregarded neighborhood institutions, including market houses, made it all but impossible for public markets to survive.

As rising values in urban real estate tempted cities to convert their downtown market property into more profitable ventures, public demand for fresh farm produce was met by markets that did not require permanent facilities. During his tenure as mayor of New York from 1954 to 1965, Robert F. Wagner showed his support for a new farmers' market at City Hall (IN-051). The market featured food grown at one of the eight "miracle gardens" sponsored by the Citizens Committee to Keep New York City Clean, Abraham and Strauss, the Sanitation Department, and the Board of Education. Wagner's support for the new farmers' markets came at the same time his administration cleared the Washington Market

IN-050. Grand Union supermarket, East Paterson, New Jersey. Gottscho-Schleisner, 1952. P&P,LC-G613-T-61187.

IN-051. Robert Wagner, Mayor, buys the first pumpkin at the new farmer's market at City Hall, New York, New York. Roger Higgins, photographer, 1958. P&P,NYWTS,Markets-Farmer's Market-Brooklyn. LC-DIG-ppmsca-12706.

IN-052. Robert Wagner, Mayor of New York, and Orville Freeman, U.S. Secretary of Agriculture, looking at the architectural rendering of the New York City Terminal Market, Hunt's Point The Bronx, New York, New York. Al Ravenna, photographer, 1962. P&P,NYWTS,Subj/Geog-Markets-Hunt's Point Market. LC-DIG-ppmsca-12699.

Robert Wagner (left), Mayor of New York from 1954 to 1965, oversaw building of the world's largest municipal wholesale market, located in the southern Bronx. Designed by Skidmore, Owings and Merrill, Hunt's Point Market opened in 1967 to replace the then-recently demolished Washington Market.

IN-053

site in Lower Manhattan for private redevelopment (see Section Seven).

Any public investment directed at new markets went to resuming construction of wholesale terminal markets—a trend that had been interrupted by the war. The USDA continued to promote model wholesale terminal markets throughout the country. With assistance from USDA marketing officials, the City of Houston opened its first terminal market in 1954; and on March 27, 1962, New York City broke ground on the $30,500,000 New York City Terminal Market—the largest produce terminal in the country, located on a 126-acre site in the Hunt's Point area of the Bronx (IN-052; see 8-047–8-053).[26]

PRESERVING HISTORIC MARKETPLACES

Some market houses from earlier eras did survive the 1960s, as a result of their historic and architectural merits. Faneuil Hall Market in Boston was recognized in 1966, when it was placed on the National Register of Historic Places. Since then, more than 100 market buildings, squares, and districts have been placed on the National Register, ranging from small neighborhood markets such as Eastern Market in Washington, D.C., to the larger Roanoke City Market Historic District.[27] These market houses operate today with differing degrees or definitions of success. South Street Seaport in New York and Faneuil Hall Market have been revived not as public markets but as festival marketplaces. These projects, largely the work of private developers, involved converting the architectural fabric of historic market districts into space for specialty shops, restaurants, pushcarts, and fast food stalls.

Two markets with long histories in their respective cities—Pike Place Market in Seattle, and Reading Terminal Market in Philadelphia—stand out as role models for having preserved their original function as well as their architectural integrity. Both were saved from demolition by grassroots campaigns to save not just the buildings but also the public market tradition.

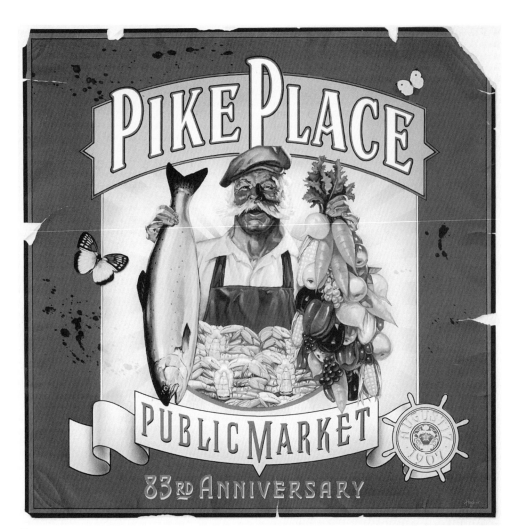

IN-054. Pike Place Public Market, 83rd Anniversary poster, Seattle, Washington. Chris Hopkins, creator, 1990. P&P,LC-DIG-ppmsca-12806(color).

IN-054

Pike Place Market had been thriving for decades until World War II, when the incarceration of Americans of Japanese ancestry, many of whom had occupied stalls at the market, prevented them from renewing their licenses. Most of the Japanese farmers who came back after the war sold their produce to commission merchants. Faced with declining sales, the Pike Place Market was partially abandoned and deteriorating when, in 1963, a city council plan proposed its total demolition. This prompted a long and successful grassroots battle to save the market. In 1973 a quasi-public corporation was established to preserve and develop the nine-acre historic market district. Pike Place Market continues today as one of the most vibrant public markets in the country and a major landmark and tourist attraction for the city of Seattle (IN-054; see 6-065–6-066).[28]

Reading Terminal Market in Philadelphia also fell on hard times after World War II, when its parent company, the Reading Railroad, experienced declining freight and passenger traffic. The market was a low priority for the company, which ultimately shut down and dismantled the market's famous cold storage facility, the largest in Philadelphia. Vendors had little choice but to provide their own refrigeration facilities or go out of business, which many did as a result of strict food safety and handling laws that required cost-

IN-055. Southwest corner of Reading Terminal Market looking north, Philadelphia, Pennsylvania. Jet Lowe, photographer, 1991. P&P,HAER,PA,51-PHILA,711-14.

IN-056. John Y's Fish Market, Reading Terminal Market, Philadelphia, Pennsylvania. Jet Lowe, photographer, 1991. P&P,HAER,PA,51-PHILA,711-15.

IN-055

IN-056

ly capital investments. By the time the Reading ceased to exist as a railroad in 1976, the market suffered from vacancies, physical neglect, and an uncertain future. Fortunately, a successful campaign run by local activists and committed market vendors won overwhelming public support to save the market and to include it in the renovation and development plans of the Pennsylvania Convention Center Authority. Reading Terminal Market survives as one of Philadelphia's most venerable institutions and the market retains a central position in the life of city (IN-055–IN-056; see 6-061–6-063).[29]

IN-057

IN-058

Cities have also paid homage to their historic marketplaces by recapturing their spirit or memory when developing new public spaces.[30] Market Square, designed by Hartman-Cox and Morris, architects, between 1984 and 1990, consists of two mixed-used residential and commercial buildings that form a hemicycle between Seventh and Ninth Streets, on the north side of Pennsylvania Avenue in Washington, D.C., just across from the National Archives (IN-057–IN-058). While the development is neither a square nor a market, its name

IN-059. Market House and City Hall, Alexandria, Virginia. Jet Lowe, photographer, 1981. P&P,HABS,VA,7-ALEX,171-8.

A weekly open air market is still held on the plaza.

IN-059

recalls Center Market, the principal public market that once stood on the location of the National Archives (7-013–7-038). Likewise, the City Hall in Alexandria, Virginia (IN-059), recalls its former market days by using the plaza for open-air markets and other community activities (see 4-026–4-027).

Not all historic market houses have enjoyed public recognition or support. Decades of neglect and a decline in both tenants and patrons left many markets standing but virtually empty by the end of the twentieth century. The O Street Market in Washington, D.C., built around 1888, was a victim of disuse and neglect. Heavy snow caused the roof to collapse in February 2003, and only three sides of the facade remain. Proposals are under way for mixed-use development of the site (IN-053).

THE PUBLIC MARKET TRADITION TODAY

People working in many disciplines and professions—economists, city planners, public policy analysts, historians, environmentalists, agriculture specialists, and others–are deeply engaged in evaluating the various benefits of public markets in modern society. The public market system has been identified as a possible antidote to the serious breakdown in contemporary food systems. The dangerous consequences of global food marketing and distribution, evident in numerous product recalls, hygiene scandals, and the threat of global pandemics, give credence to the benefits of local and regional markets. Since the public market tradition has privileged direct marketing for centuries, it holds promise for sustaining agriculture, biodiversity, and a healthy relationship among urban and rural populations, economies, and production.[31]

The rediscovered benefits of public markets are evident in the growing number of farmers' markets now operating throughout the country. Historically, a "farmers' market" comprised only the producers who sold at the public markets, usually on a seasonal basis from outdoor stands where the fees were more moderate than those of the indoor stalls. Since the late twentieth century, the terms "farmers' market" and "public market" have often been used synonymously, since both refer to markets that include a certain percentage of vendors who sell food not of their own production. Although a farmers' market, strictly defined, may allow vendors to sell second-hand goods after hours or when the season for fresh foods has ended, its primary purpose is to support local producers. A national farmers' market survey conducted by the USDA reports that there were 499 farmers' markets in 1946 and 2,863 by the year 2000—an increase of 473 percent. In 2006, the USDA reported over 3,700 farmers' markets operating in the United States.[32]

All of the market types, ranging from the simple open-air market to the more complex wholesale terminal market, have been revived and adapted to meet changing social, political, and economic conditions, while still fulfilling their mandate as public gathering points for the buying and selling of produce. As a worldwide phenomenon, the public market tradition lives on. These buildings and spaces are valued not only because they serve as healthy alternatives to supermarkets and other outlets of mass-marketed and highly processed food, but also because of their unique spirit and character—qualities that no other form of urban food retailing has yet been able to match.

NOTES

1. Theodore Morrow Spitzer and Hilary Baum, *Public Markets and Community Revitalization* (1995; repr., Washington, DC: Urban Land Institute and Project for Public Spaces, 2004), 2.

2. Spiro Kostof, *The City Assembled: The Elements of Urban Form through History*, (1992; repr., New York: W. W. Norton, 2005), 92–101; Spiro Kostof, *The City Shaped: Urban Patterns and Meanings through History* (Boston: Little, Brown), 1991, 24–25.

3. Jean-Christophe Agnew, "The Threshold of Exchange: Speculations on the Market," *Radical History Review* 21 (Fall 1979): 100–109.

4. On markets in the Athenian agora, see John M. Camp, *The Athenian Agora: Excavations in the Heart of Classical Athens* (1986; repr., London: Thames and Hudson, 1998), 14, 172–75, 181–89; Homer A. Thompson, *The Athenian Agora: A Short Guide* (Princeton, NJ: American School of Classical Studies, 1993); Homer A. Thompson and R. E. Wycherley, *The Agora of Athens: The History, Shape, and Uses of an Ancient City Center* (Princeton, NJ: American School of Classical Studies at Athens, 1972), 170–73.

5. Kostof, *The City Shaped*, 143.

6. Ibid., 142.

7. Walter M. Weiss, *The Bazaar: Markets and Merchants of the Islamic World* (London: Thames and Hudson, 1998), 39–67.

8. For market laws in antiquity, see Joan M. Frayn, *Markets and Fairs in Roman Italy: Their Social and Economic Importance from the Second Century B.C. to the Third Century A.D.* (Oxford: Clarendon Press, 1993), 121–32; in medieval England, see Kathryn A. Morrison, *English Shops and Shopping* (New Haven and London: Yale University Press, 2003), 5–6; and in more recent times, see Helen Tangires, *Public Markets and Civic Culture in Nineteenth-Century America* (Baltimore: Johns Hopkins University Press, 2003), 3–23, and William J. Novak, *The People's Welfare: Law and Regulation in Nineteenth-Century America* (Chapel Hill: University of North Carolina Press, 1996), 95–105, 290–91.

9. Nikolaus Pevsner, *A History of Building Types* (Princeton, NJ: Princeton University Press, 1976), 235–43.

10. Jeremy Taylor, "Charles Fowler: Master of Markets," *Architectural Review* (March 1964): 178–79.

11. Frances H. Steiner, *French Iron Architecture* (Ann Arbor, MI: UMI Research Press, 1984).

12. Tangires, *Public Markets and Civic Culture*, 187.

13. John Quincy Jr., *Quincy's Market: A Boston Landmark* (Boston: Northeastern University Press, 2003).

14. "Smithfield Market," *Builder*, December 29, 1866, 955; "London Central Fruit and Vegetable Market," *Builder* 38 (1880): 71–72. On the rise of the wholesale trade in Europe and its effect on the public market system in late nineteenth century, see James Schmiechen and Kenneth Carls, *The British Market Hall: A Social and Architectural History* (New Haven and London: Yale University Press, 1999), 141–42; and Tangires, *Public Markets and Civic Culture*, 185–89.

15. Andrew Lohmeier, "*Bürgerliche Gesellschaft* and Consumer Interests: The Berlin Public Market Hall Reform, 1867–1891," *Business History Review* 73 (Spring 1999): 91–113.

16. On wholesale terminal markets in Tokyo and Buenos Aires, respectively, see Theodore C. Bestor, *Tsukiji: The Fish Market at the Center of the World* (Berkeley: University of California Press, 2004), and Sonia Berjman and José Fiszelew, *El Abasto: Un barrio y un mercado* [El Abasto: A Neighborhood and a Market] (Buenos Aires: Corregidor, 1999). For the United States, see *Charles E. Magoon, The Way It Was: The Produce*

Industry in the Early Years, 1890 to 1930. An Illustrated History (Berkeley Springs, WV: Particularly Produce, 1997).

17. Tangires, *Public Markets and Civic Culture*, 26–47.

18. On the architectural development of the grocery store, see James M. Mayo, *The American Grocery Store: The Business Evolution of an Architectural Space* (Westport, CT: Greenwood Press, 1993).

19. On the rise of the dressed beef industry, see William Cronon, *Nature's Metropolis: Chicago and the Great West* (New York: W. W. Norton, 1991), 207–59; Roger Horowitz, Jeffrey M. Pilcher, and Sydney Watts, "Meat for the Multitudes: Market Culture in Paris, New York City, and Mexico City over the Long Nineteenth Century," *American Historical Review* 109, no. 4 (2004), 1055–82.

20. Helen Tangires, "Feeding the Cities: Markets and Municipal Reform in the Progressive Era," *Prologue* 29 (Spring 1997): 16–26.

21. New York City, Mayor's Market Commission, *Report of the Mayor's Market Commission New York City* (New York: Little and Ives, 1913); "Market Department Reorganized," *American City*, March 1919, 245.

22. Steven Stoll, *The Fruits of Natural Advantage: Making the Industrial Countryside in California* (Berkeley: University of California Press, 1998); Marc Linder and Lawrence Z. Zacharias, *Of Cabbages and Kings County: Agriculture and the Formation of Modern Brooklyn* (Iowa City: University of Iowa Press, 1999).

23. C. W. Short and R. Stanley-Brown, *Public Buildings: A Survey of Architecture of Projects Constructed by Federal and Other Governmental Bodies between the Years 1933 and 1939 with the Assistance of the Public Works Administration* (Washington, DC: Government Printing Office, 1939).

24. On the architectural development of the supermarket, see Richard Longstreth, *The Drive-In, the Supermarket, and the Transformation of Commercial Space in Los Angeles, 1914–1941* (Cambridge, MA: MIT Press, 1999).

25. Spitzer and Baum, *Public Markets and Community Revitalization*, 11.

26. "No Nostalgia When Packers Abandon 'Row,'" *Houston Post*, November 5, 1954; "City Starts Huge Produce Market in Bronx," *New York Times*, March 28, 1962.

27. The National Register of Historic Places, administered by the National Park Service, maintains a public database of places listed in or determined eligible for the Register. See the National Register Information System (NRIS) at www.nps.gov.

28. Alice Shorett and Murray Morgan, *The Pike Place Market: People, Politics, and Produce* (Seattle, WA: Pacific Search Press, 1982).

29. Carol M. Highsmith and James L. Holton, *Reading Terminal and Market: Philadelphia's Historic Gateway and Grand Convention Center* (Washington, DC: Chelsea Publishing, 1994); David K. O'Neil, *Reading Terminal Market: An Illustrated History* (Philadelphia: Camino Books, 2004).

30. Pamela Scott and Antoinette J. Lee, *Buildings of the District of Columbia*, Society of Architectural Historians, Buildings of the United States (New York: Oxford University Press, 1993), 188–89.

31. An important advocate for public markets in the United States is the Project for Public Spaces, Inc., in New York. It provides training and other resources for a growing international network of public markets worldwide. See www.pps.org.

32. The USDA continues to update the farmers' market survey. See www.usda.gov. On the problems associated with counting farmers' markets, see Allison Brown, "Counting Farmers Markets," *Geographical Review* 91, no. 4 (October 2001): 655–74, and Allison Brown, "Farmers' Market Research 1940–2000: An Inventory and Review," *American Journal of Alternative Agriculture* 17, no. 4 (2002): 167–76.

THE OPEN-AIR MARKETPLACE

The open-air marketplace is the most ubiquitous and universal type of public market, and it has remained rather consistent over the centuries. A town with a grid plan might establish a marketplace on the square formed by the intersection of its principal north-south and east-west axes. It might also establish satellite markets on squares formed by other major intersections. These locations take advantage of already-owned public property with good access to transportation routes and densely populated neighborhoods. Extramural sites, on the other hand, are well suited for periodic markets or fairs (1-001).

Some regional variations in form have evolved. The marketplace in Islamic cities, known as the souk or bazaar, is a business complex consisting of the mosque and an open space for the sale of fresh food and livestock, as well as streets lined with warehouses and shops devoted to the sale of goods. It may also contain public baths, lodges for traveling merchants, and fountains for ritual ablutions (1-002). Markets in China developed around temples, manors, and

41

manufacturing facilities, such as ceramic works. Outdoor vendors of produce and wares sell goods in the open, while vendors of perishable items, such as fish and flesh, occupy the sheds (1-003–1-005). Open-air markets in Latin America developed in and around plazas, occasionally under the protection of covered walkways (1-006–1-012).

1-001

1-002

The bazaar at Samarkand owed its prosperity in part to its central position on the Silk Road—an important route for goods carried between Eastern Asia and the Middle East, India, Russia, and North Africa. Traders found shade and a place to rest from their long journeys.

1-003

1-004

1-003. Market day, Seoul, Korea. George Rose, publisher, ca. 1900. P&P,LC-USZ62-86879.

1-004. Market, Chefang, China. Unidentified photographer, 1939 or 1940. P&P,FSA/OWI,LC-USW33-043109-ZC.

1-005. Market, Manchuria, Changcun. Unidentified photographer, ca. 1900–1909. P&P,LC-USZ62-47777.

1-005

1-006

1-008

1-006. *Market place, Grand Plaza, Granada, Nicaragua.* Wood engraving, 1856. P&P,LC-USZ62-60937.

1-007. Portales, Santo Domingo, Mexico City, Mexico. Globe Stereograph Company, 1906. P&P,LC-USZ62-114720.

1-008. Portales of the market of San Marcos, Aguascalientes, Mexico. William Henry Jackson, photographer, ca. 1880–1897. P&P,DETR,LC-D4-3906.

The word "portales" refers to porticoes or covered walkways.

1-009. Market Place Santa Tecla, Nueva San Salvador, El Salvador. Unidentified photographer, ca. 1909–1932. P&P,LC-USZ62-94519.

1-010. Around the Market House and Square, Mexico City, Mexico. American Stereoscopic Company, 1901. P&P,LC-USZ62-114715.

1-011. Market day, Tamazunchale, Mexico. P&P,AHC, No.400070. LC-DIG-ppmsca-12471.

1-009

1-010

1-011

1-012

1-012. Fruit market, Zanzibar. Coutinho & Sons, Mombasa, ca. 1890–1923. P&P,LC-USZ62-40650.

1-013. A busy market at Agboville, Ivory Coast. Unidentified photographer, 1959. P&P,LC-USZ62-121346.

1-014. Travel views of Morocco. Arnold Genthe, photographer, 1904. P&P,Genthe,LC-G4085-0210.

1-013

1-014

1-015

1-015. Market, Biskra, Algeria. Unidentified
photographer, ca. 1899. P&P,PC,LC-DIG-
ppmsc-05564(color).

1-016

1-017

1-018

1-016. Market, Mejex-El-Bab, Tunisia. Unidentified photographer, 1943. P&P,FSA/OWI,LC-USW3-036186-E.

This market was operated by the Allied civilian relief groups to sell at cost food, clothing, kerosene, and other goods supplied by the United States Office of Foreign Relief and Rehabilitation Operations.

1-017. Market, Mejex-El-Bab, Tunisia. Unidentified photographer, 1943. P&P,FSA/OWI,LC-USW3-036187-E.

1-018. Market, Mejex-El-Bab, Tunisia. Unidentified photographer, 1943. P&P,FSA/OWI,LC-USW3-036181-C.

1-019. Marketplace, Tiberias, Palestine. Matson Photo Service, ca. 1934–1939. P&P,LC-DIG-matpc-03301.

1-020. Marketplace, Diyarbakir, Turkey. United States Army Signal Corps, 1919. P&P,LC-USZ62-134208.

1-019

1-020

1-021. Market, Phnom Penh, Cambodia. Unidentified photographer, ca. 1925–1935. P&P,LC-USZ62-97478.

1-022. Market, Island of Luzon, Philippine Islands. Keystone View Company, 1906. P&P,LC-USZ62-80712.

50 THE OPEN-AIR MARKETPLACE

1-023. Market, Baguio, Philippine Islands. Unidentified photographer, ca. 1920–1925. P&P,LC-USZ61-2091.

1-024. Attending market in winter, Moscow, Russia. Keystone View Company, 1919. P&P,LC-USZ62-69977.

1-025. Traders' wares in the Tartar market, St. Petersburg, Russia. Unidentified photographer, 1903. P&P,LC-USZ62-118968.

1-023

1-024

1-025

1-026. Peasants selling bread, milk, eggs, etc., Russia. Unidentified photographer, 1910. P&P,LC-USZ62-36538.

1-027. Jewish Market, Moscow, Russia. Unidentified photographer, before 1944. P&P,LC-DIG-ggbain-09753.

1-028. New Market and Bourse, Amsterdam, The Netherlands. Unidentified photographer, ca. 1890–1900. P&P,PCHROM,LC-USZC4-2122(color).

I-027

I-028

1-029

1-029. Market Square, Château des Comptes, Ghent, Belgium. P&P,USZ62-4004(color).

1-030. Vegetable market and bridge over the river Shannon (E.), Athlone, central Ireland. Underwood & Underwood, 1903. P&P,LC-USZ62-127367.

1-031. The market place, Viborg, Finland. Underwood & Underwood, 1897. P&P,LC-USZ62-92677.

1-030

1-031

1-032

1-033

1-032. Marketplace, Argos, Greece. H. C. White Company, 1901. P&P,LC-USZ62-65925.

1-033. The great Saturday market in Helsingfors, Finland. Keystone View Company, 1905. P&P,LC-USZ62-120647.

1-034. Marketplace, Argos, Greece. Underwood & Underwood, 1903. P&P,LC-USZ62-65892.

1-034

1-035

1-036

1-037

1-035. Marketplace, Sparta, Greece. Underwood & Underwood, 1907. P&P,LC-USZ62-66135.

1-036. Open-air market in front of the silk exchange, Valencia, Spain. J. Laurent, photographer, ca. 1860–1880. P&P,LC-USZ62-108724.

1-037. Working people at market, Postigo del Aceite, Seville, Spain. Underwood & Underwood, 1908. P&P,LC-USZ62-73735.

1-038. Marketplace, St. John, Antigua, West Indies. H. C. White Company, 1902. P&P,LC-USZ62-65530.

1-039. Market, Mandeville, Jamaica. H. C. White Company, 1904. P&P,LC-USZ62-91667.

1-038

1-039

1-040

1-040. Champlain Market, Quebec, Canada. Unidentified photographer, 1899. P&P, Souvenir Viewbooks-Foreign-Canada-Quebec of To-Day. LC-DIG-ppmsca-12317.

1-041. Jacques Cartier Square, Montreal, Canada. Unidentified photographer, 1900. P&P,DETR,LC-D4-12507.

1-042. Market square looking northeast, Cleburne, Texas. P&P,LC-USZ62-16199.

1-041

1-042

THE MARKET AND THE STATE

State regulation of the trade in fresh food has its roots in antiquity. Regulated public markets were critical to the survival of the town because without them, unfair commercial practices could jeopardize the public welfare. Local government enacted laws that were intended to protect citizens from forestalling (buying products before they reached the market), engrossing (monopolizing the market with the intent of driving up prices), and the selling of food that was spoiled or short in weight or measure. To facilitate this responsibility, markets were located near the seat of authority—either the town hall or courthouse—a tradition still practiced. In some cases, markets and government offices share the same buildings (see Section 4).

1-043. Hauptplatz and market, Grosswardein, Hungary, Austro-Hungary. Unidentified photographer, ca. 1890–1900. P&P,PCHROM,LC-DIG-ppmsc-09483(color).

1-043

1-044

1-045

1-046

1-047

1-044. Market Square and Town Hall, Arras (Pas-de-Calais), France. Unidentified photographer, ca. 1914. P&P,Foreign Geog File France-Arras(Pas-de-Calais). LC-DIG-ppmsca-12309.

1-045. Hotel de Ville and market place, Aachen, the Rhine, Germany. Unidentified photographer, ca. 1890–1900. P&P,PCHROM,LC-DIG-ppmsca-00764(color).

1-046. Market place, Breslau, Silesia, Germany (i.e., Wroclaw, Poland). Unidentified photographer, ca. 1890–1900. P&P,PCHROM,LC-DIG-ppmsca-01065(color).

1-047. Market, Altstadt, Dresden, Saxony, Germany. Unidentified photographer, ca. 1890–1900. P&P,PCHROM,LC-DIG-ppmsca-00946(color).

1-048

1-048. The market place and side of Hotel de Ville, Halle, Saxony, Germany. Unidentified photographer, ca. 1890–1900. P&P,PCHROM,LC-DIG-ppmsca-01007(color).

1-049. Market place, Halle, Saxony, Germany. Unidentified photographer, ca. 1890–1900. P&P,PCHROM,LC-DIG-ppmsca-01006(color).

The marketplace is dominated by the Marienkirche, with its four slender spires, and by the massive fifteenth-century Red Tower.

1-049

1-050. Market place and Hotel de Ville, Leipzig, Saxony, Germany. Unidentified photographer, ca. 1890–1900. P&P,PCHROM,LC-DIG-ppmsca-00965(color).

1-051. Hauptmarkt, Nuremburg, Germany. Unidentified photographer, ca. 1860–1890. P&P,LC-USZ62-109034.

The city embellished the market square in the seventeenth century with arcades. The Rathaus, or City Hall, stands in the background.

1-050

1-051

1-052

1-052. Market place, Magdeburg, Saxony, Germany. Unidentified photographer, ca. 1890–1900. P&P,PCHROM,LC-DIG-ppmsca-01010(color).

1-053. The Great Market, Nijmegen, Holland. Unidentified photographer, ca. 1890–1910. P&P,PCHROM,LC-DIG-ppmsc-05830(color).

1-053

1-054. Courthouse and market, public square, Nashville, Tennessee. Unidentified photographer, 1892. P&P,LC-USZ62-74298.

1-055. Market Square, Washington, Georgia. Unidentified photographer, after 1908. P&P,SSF.Markets-GA-Washington. LC-DIG-ppmsca-12322.

The building in the background is the Wilkes County Courthouse.

1-054

1-055

MARKERS AND MONUMENTS

A long-standing tradition in urban design is the use of markers to accent a vista or to fix the space of a formal square. The repertory of markers located in marketplaces includes fountains, triumphal arches, commemorative columns, statues, and towers. Fountains, of course, double as ornaments and sources of public water. Likewise, belfries and clock towers not only give visual authority to the marketplace but may also function to signal the hours of trade.

1-056. Market place and Bismarck's Fountain, Jena, Thuringia, Germany. Unidentified photographer, ca. 1890–1900. P&P,PCHROM,LC-DIG-ppmsca-01105(color).

1-056

1-057. The New Market Place, Vienna, Austro-Hungary. Unidentified photographer, ca. 1880s. P&P,LC-USZ62-70896.

The fountain Providentia-Brunnen, built 1737–1739, was designed by Georg Raphael Donner.

1-058. The market fountain, Carlsbad, Bohemia, Austro-Hungary. Unidentified photographer, ca. 1890–1900. P&P,PCHROM,LC-DIG-ppmsc-09289(color).

1-057

1-058

1-059

1-060

1-059. Market, Platz Am Hof, Vienna, Austro-Hungary. Unidentified photographer, ca. 1890–1900. P&P,PCHROM,LC-DIG-ppm-sc-09211(color).

Two bronze sculptures dominated the square. The tall monument in the background is the extant Mariensäule, or Column of the Holy Mary, by Balthasar Herold, from the seventeenth century. The equestrian statue is a monument to Field Marshall Count Joseph Radetzky, by Caspar von Zumbusch, from 1886 to 1892. It was moved in 1912 to the then newly built Ministry of War, where it stands today.

1-060. Marketplace, Bremen, Germany. Unidentified photographer, ca. 1890–1900. P&P,PCHROM,LC-USZC4-2033(color).

Medieval Germanic cities customarily erected statues of Knight Roland in their main squares as a symbol of civic rights, including the privilege to hold markets. This one, built in 1404, still stands.

1-061. Marketplace, Ripon, England. P&P, Foreign Geog File-England-Ripon. LC-DIG-ppmsca-12300.

1-062. Marketplace, Honfleur (Calvados), France. From Ralph Adams Cram, *Farm Houses, Manor Houses, Minor Chateaux and Small Churches from the Eleventh to the Sixteenth Centuries in Normandy, Brittany and Other Parts of France* (1917), p. 82. Gen. Coll.,NA1041.F3. LC-DIG-ppmsca-12645.

1-061

1-062

1-063. Market cross, Kirkby Lonsdale, England. P&P,Foreign-Geog-File-England-Kirkby-Lonsdale. LC-DIG-ppmsca-12298.

1-064. Poultry cross, Salisbury, England. P&P,Foreign-Geog-File-England-Salisbury. LC-DIG-ppmsca-12301.

1-063

1-064

1-065

1-065. Minaret in a market quarter, Aleppo (Haleb) and environs, Syria. American Colony (Jerusalem), Photo Department, ca. 1910–1920. P&P,LC-DIG-matpc-02160.

Similar to a bell or clock tower, the minaret—or tower in Islamic architecture from which the faithful are called to prayer—is located in the market district in order to reach a wide audience. It also gives visual authority to the marketplace.

1-066. City cross, Winchester, England. P&P,Foreign Geog File-England-Winchester(color). LC-DIG-ppmsca-12302.

1-067. Old cross and stocks, Lymm, England. P&P,Foreign Geog File-England-Lymm. LC-DIG-ppmsca-12299.

City Cross, Winchester.

1-066

1-067

FURNITURE AND FIXTURES

Open-air markets typically are located on sites that are also used for other public functions when the market is closed. In order to keep these spaces flexible, cities minimize the use of permanent furniture and fixtures. Vendors, therefore, provide their own furniture, such as trestle tables, stools, crates, and chairs. They may pitch tents or bring umbrellas for protection from the elements, or they fabricate makeshift stalls that are removed at the end of the day.

1-068. The fruit market, looking west over the great market place, Vienna, Austria. Underwood & Underwood, 1902. P&P,LC-USZ62-75163.

1-068

1-069. Travel views of Europe. Arnold Genthe, photographer, ca. 1904–1938. P&P,LC-G395-T-0080.

1-070. Mercado, Plaza de Armas, Iglesia de la Compania, Cuzco, Peru. Unidentified photographer, ca. 1907. P&P,LC-USZ62-133406.

1-071. Tree-lined marketplace, Lubeck, Germany. Unidentified photographer, ca. 1890–1900. P&P,PCHROM,LC-DIG-ppmsca-00666(color).

1-069

1-070

1-071

1-072

1-073

1-074

1-072. Marketplace at Aculxameca, Mexico. Unidentified photographer. P&P,AHC,LC-USH52-162.

1-073. The Market, Freiburg, Baden, Germany. Unidentified photographer, ca. 1890–1900. P&P,PCHROM,LC-DIG-ppmsca-00303(color).

1-074. The plaza on market day, Taxco, Mexico. Gordon C. Abbott, photographer, ca. 1925–1949. P&P,LC-USZ62-125836.

These vendors have set up beneath the shade of some trees.

1-075. Central market, Petrazavodsk, Russia. William C. Brumfield, photographer, 1991. P&P,Brum,LC-DIG-ppmsca-01329(color).

1-076. Berger nomads in the walled market place at Timbuktu, Sudanese Republic (Mali). Unidentified photographer, ca. 1950–1961. P&P,NYWTS,LC-USZ62-132423.

The market stands are covered with goatskins, wooden flaps, and woven mats.

1-077. Market, Military Plaza, San Antonio, Texas. E. K. Sturdevant, photographer, 1887. P&P,LC-USZ62-24772.

1-078. Central market, Petrazavodsk, Russia. William C. Brumfield, photographer, 1991. P&P,Brum,LC-DIG-ppmsca-01328(color).

Some vendors use wooden crates for counters and seats. Others sell from permanent concrete benches. Lining the perimeter of the market square are makeshift wooden stalls with upright posts supporting corrugated metal roofs.

1-076

1-075

1-077

1-078

SPECIALIZED AND SEASONAL MARKETS

Most public markets are general marts, where a variety of foodstuffs are sold on a regular basis. Certain kinds of markets exist, nonetheless, for the sale of items that require special handling. Fish markets, for example, might be located along a port or directly on the beach, in order to exploit a waterfront location. Livestock markets require large open spaces and, in general, were held on designated days in the market square until the early twentieth century. They are located more typically on the outskirts of town in order to avoid driving animals through the streets. Other markets are dictated by the seasons; they include special places and times for the sale of hay, wheat, cotton, flowers, melons, cheese, and holiday greens.

1-079. Vedute Pittoriche. No. 1. *Veduta della pescheria di Palermo in Sicilia (View of the fish market in Palermo, Sicily)*. I. De Vegni, engraver. P&P,PGA-DeVegni,1. Veduta della pescheria di Palermo in Sicilia(B size). LC-DIG-ppmsca-12156.

1-079

1-080. Fish market, Bergen, Norway. Unidentified photographer, ca. 1890–1900. P&P,PCHROM,LC-DIG-ppmsc-06108(color).

1-081. Fish market, Chioggia, Italy. Unidentified photographer, ca. 1890–1900 P&P,PCHROM,LC-DIG-ppmsc-06708(color).

1-082. A fish market in Manila, Philippine Islands. Unidentified photographer, 1905. P&P,LC-USZ62-86148.

1-083. Fish market, Chemulpo, Korea. American Stereoscopic Company, 1904. P&P,LC-USZ62-72538.

1-080

1-081

1-082

1-083

1-084

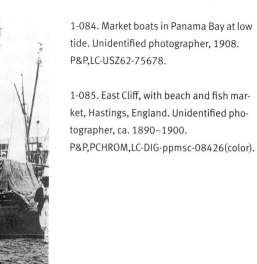

1-084. Market boats in Panama Bay at low tide. Unidentified photographer, 1908. P&P,LC-USZ62-75678.

1-085. East Cliff, with beach and fish market, Hastings, England. Unidentified photographer, ca. 1890–1900. P&P,PCHROM,LC-DIG-ppmsc-08426(color).

1-085

1-086. Fish market, Portugal. P&P,Foreign Geog File-Portugal. LC-DIG-ppmsca-12307.

1-087. *Dutch Market Boats*. Charles A. Platt, etcher, 1888. P&P,LC-USZ62-91340.

1-086

1-087

1-088

1-089

1-090

1-088. Fish and Oyster Market, New Bern, North Carolina. M. E. Whitehurst & Company, ca. 1900–1950. P&P,LC-USZ62-98925.

1-089. Jerusalem (El-Kouds), approach to the city. Cattle market in lower pool of Gihon. American Colony (Jerusalem), Photo Department, ca. 1910–1920. P&P,LC-DIG-matpc-00859.

1-090. The Great Bell Market in the Fair, Nijni-Novgorod, Russia, H. C. White Company, stereographer, 1902. P&P,LC-USZ62-69993.

1-091. Cattle market, Galway, Ireland. Underwood & Underwood, 1901. P&P, LC-USZ62-115283.

1-092. Horse market, South Omaha, Nebraska. Bee Publishing Company, 1914. P&P, LC-USZ62-52768 and -52769.

1-093. Horse market in Cheapside Public Square, Lexington, Kentucky. Keystone View Company, 1920. P&P, LC-USZ62-72860.

1-092

1-091

1-093

1-094

1-094. Wheat market, Offerle, Kansas. Unidentified photographer, 1916. P&P, LC-USZ62-61198.

1-095. Bales of cotton on horse-drawn wagons in the market square, Montgomery, Alabama. Unidentified photographer, 1917. P&P, LC-USZ62-88539.

1-096. Flower market at the Palais de Justice, Paris, France. P&P, LC-USZ62-71263.

1-097. Easter Flower Market, Union Square, New York, New York. P&P, LC-DIG-ggbain-03257.

1-098. Easter Flower Market, Union Square, New York, New York. P&P, LC-DIG-ggbain-03259.

1-095

1-096

1-097

1-098

1-099

1-100

1-101

1-102

1-099. Harbor scene, Salvador, Brazil. P&P,AHC,LC-USH52-406.

1-100. Flower vendor's Easter display, New York, New York.
Unidentified photographer, 1904. P&P,DETR,LC-D4-9204.

1-101. Old clothes market, Bridgemarket(?), New York, New York.
P&P,LC-USZ62-72442.

1-102. Market scene along waterfront, with piles of pineapples
and watermelons in foreground, Tampico, Mexico. Eugenio B.
Downing, photographer, ca. 1890–1930. P&P,LC-USZ62-114770.

1-103. Growers lining up for the inspection of buyers, watermelon market, Stockdale, Texas. Unidentified photographer, 1938. P&P,NYWTS Subj/Geog-Watermelons. AP/Wide World Photos.

opposite
1-104. Central Market, Rome, Italy. Albert Blasetti, photographer, ca. 1954, Albert Blasett/Corbis. P&P,NYWTS Subj/Geog Italy-Rome-Markets. LC-DIG-ppmsca-12690.

1-105. Central Market, Rome, Italy. Unidentified photographer, ca. 1954. P&P,NYWTS Subj/Geog Italy-Rome-Markets. LC-DIG-ppmsca-12691.

1-106. Unloading watermelons at the farmers' market, Washington, D.C. Marjory Collins, photographer, 1942. P&P,FSA/OWI,LC-USF34-100626-E.

1-107. Boatload of watermelons, Norfolk, Virginia(?). Theodor Horydczak, photographer, ca. 1920–1950. P&P,Hory,LC-H822-T-B06-015.

1-103

1-104

1-106

1-105

1-107

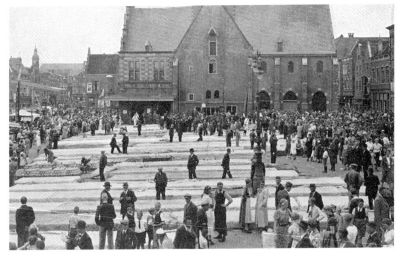

1-108

1-109

1-108. Cheese market, Alkmaar, The Netherlands.
P&P,Postcards,PR 06(AA) CN 038,Box2. LC-DIG-
ppmsca-12812.

1-109. Cheese porters, Alkmaar, The Netherlands.
P&P,Postcards,PR 06(AA) CN 038,Box2. LC-DIG-
ppmsca-12811.

1-110. Vendors selling greens under trees at the old Center
Market, Washington, D.C. Unidentified photographer, ca.
1880–1900. P&P,LC-DIGppmsc-09957.

1-110

1-111. Christmas tree market, New York City, New York. Unidentified photographer, 1903. P&P,DETR,LC-D4-9148.

1-112. Christmas trees for sale at the market, Providence, Rhode Island. Jack Delano, photographer, 1940. P&P,FSA/OWI,LC-USF34-042664-D.

1-111

1-112

STREET MARKETS

Street markets are characterized by their linear expansion on a sidewalk, in a street or vacant lot, on a bridge, or underneath the approach to a bridge. Vendors sit or stand, selling from stalls, small portable stands, wagons, pushcarts, and trucks. These elongated marketplaces usually are located on publicly owned land, making them very economical to establish. They are also flexible and easy to expand, since they are not constrained by permanent structures.

Despite, or perhaps because of, the absence of architectural definition, street markets are subject to the strict allocation of space. In the early imperial capitals of China, for example, markets were inscribed rigidly on the two sides of the central ceremonial axis. Similar in practice were elaborate and lengthy ordinances in nineteenth-century Philadelphia that dictated, among other things, the strict placement of vendors at the High Street Market.

A demand for direct marketing between producer and consumer is one of the driving forces behind the establishment of street markets. During World War I, food shortages and high food prices raised awareness of the benefits of direct marketing, forcing many cities to establish what were more commonly referred to as curb markets (2-027–2-031). A curb market is a designated place, along a street curb or on a vacant lot, where market wagons and trucks belonging to farmers and hucksters can be accommodated. The street curb adjacent to the market house is often used for this purpose.

The pushcart market also has its own historical evolution in the United States, most notably in New York City (2-032–2-056). It evolved from the centuries-old practice of itinerant peddlers selling from baskets or small portable stands. New York's pushcart markets rose to prominence beginning in the 1880s, when high residential densities in certain immigrant neighborhoods encouraged peddlers to gather and sell continuously from single locations. Likewise, European immigrants found the neighborhood-based pushcart market a familiar cultural and linguistic setting in which to earn a living.

Despite the availability of alternative food outlets, street markets are still very much a part of the urban landscape throughout the modern world, as they continue to provide an important means of subsistence for farmers and other food vendors. Many consumers, too, remain devoted to street markets because of traditional shopping practices, the markets' special ambience, and the variety and types of food that are available.

2-001. Street market, Mexico. William Henry Jackson, photographer, 1884 or 1885. P&P,LC-USZ62-108570.

opposite
2-002. Market, La Union, El Salvador. B. L. Singley (Keystone View Company), stereographer, 1902. P&P,LC-USZ62-80219.

2-003. Street scene in the market at San Salvador, El Salvador, where milling stones for grinding flour are sold. P&P,Foreign Geog File-Salvador-San Salvador. LC-DIG-ppmsca-12314.

2-004. Street market, Hong Kong, China. Carleton H. Graves, publisher, 1902. P&P,LC-USZC4-6735(color).

2-005. The vegetable market, Nazareth, Palestine. American Colony (Jerusalem), Photo Department, ca. 1920–1933. P&P,LC-DIG-matpc-00217.

2-001

2-002

2-004

2-003

2-005

2-006

2-007

2-006. Fruit and vegetable stalls at De Bab–Segma, Fez, Morocco. Unidentified photographer, ca. 1917. P&P,LC-USZC4-2175.

Rows of small booths, open to the street, are a typical feature of the bazaar.

2-007. Arab market, Jerusalem. American Colony (Jerusalem), Photo Department, 1925. P&P,LC-DIG-matpc-04752.

Folding wooden doors or shutters protected shops from the sun during market hours and provided security when closed.

2-008. Melon vendor, Samarkand. Sergei Mikhailovich Prokudin-Gorskii, photographer, ca. 1905–1915. P&P,Prok,LC-DIG-ppmsc-03949(color).

2-008

2-009

2-010

2-011

2-009. The Hauptstrasse and market, Debreczin (i.e., Debrecen), Austro-Hungary. Unidentified photographer, ca. 1890–1900. P&P,PCHROM,LC-DIG-ppmsc-09480(color).

2-010. Market stalls beside old powder magazine, Irkutsk, Russia. Unidentified photographer, 1885 or 1886. P&P,LC-USZ62-123336.

2-011. Street market, Tibet. Unidentified photographer, ca. 1930–1933. P&P,LC-USZ62-75949.

2-012

2-012. Market, Nice, France. Unidentified photographer, ca. 1890–1900. P&P,PCHROM,LC-DIG-ppmsc-05965(color).

2-013. Nasch Market, Vienna, Austro-Hungary. Unidentified photographer, ca. 1890–1900. P&P,PCHROM,LC-DIG-ppmsc-09222(color).

2-014. Bosen Torgglhaus and fruit market, Tyrol, Austro-Hungary. Unidentified photographer, ca. 1890–1900. P&P,PCHROM,LC-DIG-ppmsc-09609(color).

2-014

2-013

2-015. Market Day, Tannton, England. Unidentified photographer, ca. 1890–1900. P&P,PCHROM,LC-DIG-ppmsc-08886(color).

2-016. Market, Yarmouth, England. Unidentified photographer, ca. 1890–1900. P&P,PCHROM,LC-DIG-ppmsc-09028(color).

2-017. Travel views of Europe. Arnold Genthe, photographer, ca. 1904–1938. P&P,LC-G395-T-0022.

2-015

2-016

2-017

2-018

2-019

2-020

2-018. Travel views of Europe. Arnold Genthe, photographer, ca. 1904–1938. P&P,LC-G395-T-0222.

2-019. City Hall and street market, Baltimore, Maryland. W. M. Chase (American Views), stereographer. P&P,LC-USZ6-1163.

2-020. Buying fish in the market, Chinatown, San Francisco, California. C. L. Wasson (International Stereograph Company), photographer, 1906. P&P,LC-USZ62-70345.

2-021

2-021. Street market, Paris, France.
Unidentified photographer, ca. 1920.
P&P,LC-USZ62-79278.

These vendors brought their goods in large
baskets that doubled as counters.

2-022

2-022. Women buying and selling items along a street, Hanoi, Vietnam. Photoprint by Quoc-Gia Viet-Nam, 1950 or 1951. P&P,LC-USZ62-86115.

2-023. Street market, Rio de Janeiro, Brazil. Claudia Andujar, photographer, 1962. LC-DIG-ppmsca-12350.

2-024. Street market, Rio de Janeiro, Brazil. Claudia Andujar, photographer, 1962. LC-DIG-ppmsca-12352.

2-025. Fish vendors at a street market, Rio de Janeiro, Brazil. Claudia Andujar, photographer, 1962. LC-DIG-ppmsca-12353.

2-026. Fruit vendor at a street market, Rio de Janeiro, Brazil. Claudia Andujar, photographer, 1962. LC-DIG-ppmsca-12351.

2-023

2-024

2-025

2-026

CURB MARKETS

Curb markets are the simplest type of street market, can be started with little expense, can be moved easily if the location is found to be faulty, and can test public support for direct marketing between producer and consumer. They were particularly popular in the United States during World War I, when federal and state departments of agriculture promoted them as a means to stabilize food prices and to deal quickly with the distribution of perishables. In 1913 two and a half miles of streets in Cleveland, Ohio, were lined with 1,300 farmers and 400 hucksters; and about 1,500 wagons attended curb markets daily in Baltimore, Maryland, and Montreal, Canada.

2-027

2-027. Vegetable vendors along Constitution Avenue near Tenth Street, adjacent to Center Market, Washington, D.C. Unidentified photographer, ca. 1908. P&P,Goode,G 1053X. LC-DIG-ppmsca-12476.

2-028. Sixth Street Market, Richmond, Virginia. Unidentified photographer, 1908. P&P,DETR,LC-USZ62-112762.

2-028

2-029

2-030

2-029. Vendors selling melons, corn, and squash, Sixth Street Market, Richmond, Virginia. Unidentified photographer, 1908. P&P,DETR,LC-USZ62-112763.

2-030. Market, Indianapolis, Indiana. Lewis Wickes Hine, photographer, 1908. P&P,NCLC,LC-DIG-nclc-03213.

2-031. Street market, Wilmington, Delaware. Lewis Wickes Hine, photographer, 1920. P&P,NCLC,LC-DIG-nclc-03569.

On market days, two to three hundred farmers crowded King Street from Second to Ninth streets. They backed their wagons up to the curb, left their horses at nearby livery stables, and raised the wagon shafts so that they would not project into the street.

2-031

PUSHCART MARKETS

In 1905 there were over 4,000 pushcart vendors in New York, primarily of Irish, Italian, Greek, and Jewish descent. By 1929 the number grew to 7,860 pushcarts distributed over 53 pushcart market zones. New York's pushcart markets were at the whim of civic, political, and business interests throughout the twentieth century. During World War I the city inaugurated several new pushcart markets underneath the approaches to the Manhattan, Williamsburg, and Queensboro bridges (2-033–2-034) in an effort to deal with sudden disruptions in food distribution. However, in the 1930s Mayor Fiorello La Guardia abolished many street markets and relocated the pushcart peddlers to newly constructed enclosed market houses (see 6-090–6-97).

2-032. Street market, Mulberry Street, New York, New York. Unidentified photographer, ca. 1900. P&P,DETR,LC-USZC4-1584(color).

2-032

2-033

2-034

2-035

2-033. Italian neighborhood with street market, Mulberry Street, New York, New York. Unidentified photographer, ca. 1900–1910. P&P,DETR,LC-D418-9350.

2-034. Sunday morning at Orchard and Rivington, New York City, New York. Bain News Service, ca. 1915. P&P,LC-USZ62-72444.

2-035. Banana sales at an open-air market. Unidentified photographer, ca. 1900. P&P,LC-USZ62-131516.

2-036

2-037

2-038

2-036. A scene in the ghetto, Hester Street, New York, New York, 1902. Benjamin J. Falk, photographer. P&P PAN US GEOG – New York no. 197 (E size). LC-USZ62-51301 and 51302.

2-037. Pushcart market, East Side, New York City, New York. Unidentified photographer, ca. 1915. P&P,LC-USZ62-99961.

2-038. Bridgemarket, New York, New York. Unidentified photographer, ca. 1916. P&P,SSF:Markets.

2-039

2-040. Street market, New York, New York. Unidentified photographer, 1938. Corbis. P&P,NYWTS,Subj/Geog-Markets-General. LC-DIG-ppm-sca-12694.

2-041. Belmont Avenue pushcart market, Brooklyn, New York, New York. Alan Fisher, photographer, 1939. P&P,NYWTS,Subj/Geog-Markets-Push Cart. LC-DIG-ppmsca-12717.

2-039. *Eastside, New York.* Woodcut. Albert Potter, artist, ca. 1931–1935. P&P,LC-DIG-ppmsc-00779. Courtesy of the Estate of the Artist and the Susan Teller Gallery, NY.

2-040

2-041

2-042

2-043

2-044

2-042. Belmont Avenue pushcart market, New York, New York. Alan Fisher, photographer, 1939. P&P,NYWTS,Subj/Geog-Markets-Push Cart. LC-DIG-ppmsca-12714.

2-043. Al Rabinowitz, pushcart market, Brooklyn, New York, New York. Unidentified photographer, 1940. P&P,NYWTS,Subj/Geog-Markets-Push Cart. LC-DIG-ppmsca-12713.

2-044. Benny Brodsky, pushcart market, Brooklyn, New York, New York. Unidentified photographer, 1940. P&P,NYWTS,Subj/Geog-Markets-Push Cart. LC-DIG-ppmsca-12715.

2-045. Belmont Avenue pushcart market, Brooklyn, New York, New York. Ben Schiff, photographer, 1958. P&P,NYWTS,Subj/Geog-Markets-Push Cart. LC-DIG-ppmsca-12716.

2-046. Moe, the Vegetable Man, Brooklyn pushcart market, New York, New York. Ben Schiff, photographer, 1958. P&P,NYWTS,Subj/Geog-Markets-Push Cart. LC-DIG-ppmsca-12711.

2-045

2-046

2-047

2-048

2-049

2-047. Pushcart market, New York, New York. Ben Schiff, photographer, 1958. P&P,NYWTS,Subj/Geog-Markets-Push Cart. LC-DIG-ppmsca-12720.

Caption reads, "Two aged women prod, pinch and pick vegetables from a tempting display of the very freshest farm produce. They could do the same in a modern self-service market but many long-time outdoor shoppers say, 'Why change the habits of a lifetime?'"

2-048. Belmont Avenue pushcart market, Brooklyn, New York, New York. Roger Higgins, photographer, ca. 1960. P&P,NYWTS,Subj/Geog-Markets-Push Cart. LC-DIG-ppmsca-12709.

2-049. Street market, New York, New York. Unidentified photographer, 1960. Corbis. P&P,NYWTS,Subj/Geog-Markets-General. LC-DIG-ppmsca-12695.

2-050. Belmont Avenue pushcart market, Brooklyn, New York, New York. C. M. Stieglitz, photographer.
P&P,NYWTS,Subj/Geog-Markets-Push Cart. LC-DIG-ppmsca-12707.

2-051. Belmont Avenue pushcart market, Brooklyn, New York, New York. Alan Fisher, photographer.
P&P,NYWTS,Subj/Geog-Markets-Push Cart. LC-DIG-ppmsca-12721.

2-050

2-051

2-052

2-052. Charles Catalano cleaning fish, Hester and Mott streets, New York, New York. Phyllis Twachtman, photographer. P&P,NYWTS,Subj/Geog-Markets-General. LC-DIG-ppmsca-12696.

2-053. Pushcart market, Prospect Place, between Saratoga and Howard avenues, Brooklyn, New York, New York. Roger Higgins, photographer. LC-DIG-ppmsca-12710.

According to the caption, Albert S. Pacetta (center), Commissioner of Markets, gave official notice that the Brooklyn pushcart market would be closed in a few days.

2-053

2-054

2-054. Belmont Avenue pushcart market, Brooklyn, New York,
New York. Roger Higgins, photographer, 1962.
P&P,NYWTS,Subj/Geog-Markets-Push Cart. LC-DIG-ppmsca-
12712.

Caption reads, "Peddler repeats part of a fading pushcart drama
on a three-block stretch of the Belmont Avenue outdoor market.
Pushcarts are disappearing in the face of supermarkets."

2-055. Albert S. Pacetta, Commissioner, New York City,
Department of Markets, shakes hands with vendor Molly Zeidman
at the Belmont Street pushcart market. Orlando Fernandez, photographer. P&P,NYWTS,Subj/Geog-New York City-
Markets,Department of. LC-DIG-ppmsca-12732.

2-056. Pushcart market, Brooklyn, New York, New York. Roger
Higgins, photographer, 1964. P&P,NYWTS,Subj/Geog-Markets-
Push Cart. LC-DIG-ppmsca-12719.

2-055

2-056

STREET VENDORS

In general, street vendors fall under the same jurisdiction as vendors in the public markets. The local government controls or prohibits their activities through licensing, ordinances, and regulations designed to maintain public health, safety, and welfare. Throughout the centuries street vendors have provided an important public service for people who are not able to get to market, by offering fruits and vegetables, bread, and milk to the elderly, infirm, or disabled. The public also benefits from the convenience of procuring quick and inexpensive meals or snacks near the workplace.

Traditionally, street vending has been an important occupational safety net. Municipal market laws in nineteenth-century America, for example, limited holders of peddler licenses to the elderly, widowed, disabled, and indigent who otherwise had few options to support themselves or their families. Street vending is still a public service and continues to be an important sector of the economy in many societies today.

The very nature of the trade demands that street vendors assume responsibility for their own environment. With no permanent place, equipment, or furnishings from which to sell, they must figure out ways to maintain their mobility, protect themselves and their goods from inclement weather, and develop their own merchandising techniques. Carts and signs are usually handmade, goods are rigged masterfully for safe transport, displays are creative and attractive, and costumes and gear tend to be colorful and flamboyant.

Perhaps the most universal and timeless features of street vendors are their cries. These distinctive songs or bawls are meant to draw the attention of potential customers, and they also identify the type of goods and wares for sale. Street cries contribute to the cacophony and commercial clamor of the marketplace—at times becoming so widespread as to demand legislation to restrict or forbid them. Street cries from many parts of the world have been published; some are available in recorded form at the Library of Congress (e.g., *The Street Cries of Charleston*, MPBRS, Society for Preservation of the Spiritual 13 mx [78A]).

ON FOOT

Vendors on foot either sell door to door or walk the streets looking for customers. They carry their merchandise with the aid of baskets, bundles, containers, trays, or yokes. Some vendors balance goods on their heads or, as in the case of live poultry, carry them in their arms.

3-001. New River Water. Engraving by Mauron. From Pierce Tempest, *The Cryes of London Drawne after the Life*, London (1711), plate 61. P&P,LC-USZ62-78104.

opposite
3-002. Broom vendor, Naples, Italy. Fotografia Giorgio Conrad, 1869. P&P,LC-USZ62-122523.

3-003. Bread vendor, Peru. Watercolor, ca. 1830–1849. P&P,LC-USZC4-440(color).

3-004. Street vendors, Charleston, South Carolina. Kilburn Brothers, stereographers, 1879. P&P,LC-USZ62-68072.

3-005. Bread vendor, Algeria. Neurdein frères, photographers, ca. 1860–1890. P&P,LC-DIG-ppmsca-04763.

3-001

3-006

3-007

3-008

3-006. Milk delivery in Jamaica. B. I. Singley (Keystone View Company), photographer, 1900. P&P,LC-USZ62-65575.

3-007. White-robed pottery peddlers on the streets of Seoul, Korea. W. S. Smith (Standard Scenic Company), photographer, 1906. P&P,LC-USZ62-72539.

3-008. A fish peddler, Aguadilla, Puerto Rico. Strohmeyer & Wyman, stereographers, 1900. P&P,LC-USZ62-65591.

3-009. Southern fish vendor, probably Augusta, Georgia. Unidentified photographer, 1903. P&P,DETR,LC-D4-16452.

3-010. The Walking Chocolate Man, Brussels, Belgium. Underwood and Underwood, ca. 1920–1930. P&P, SSF: Peddlers and Peddling. LC-DIG-ppmsca-12324.

The long stick at the bottom of the tank helps keep the load off the man's shoulder.

3-011. Young street vendors in front of meat stalls, Ponta Delgado, Portugal. Unidentified photographer, ca. 1880–1900. P&P, Foreign Geog File-Portugal-Ponta Delgado. LC-DIG-ppmsca-12308.

3-012. A man, wearing a fez, selling drinks from an ornate, portable, samovar-like dispenser in the Syrian Quarter of New York City, New York. Unidentified photographer, ca. 1910–1920. P&P,LC-USZ62-37780.

3-013. Gus Strateges, celery vendor, Center Market, Washington, D.C. Lewis Wickes Hine, photographer, 1912. P&P,NCLC,LC-DIG-nclc-05496.

"10:30 p.m. At Center Market. 11 yr. old Celery Vendor Gus Strateges, 212 Jackson Hall Alley. He sold until 11 p.m. and was out again Sunday morning selling papers and gum. Has been in this country only a year and a half."

3-011

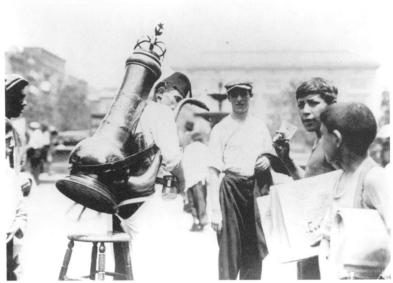
3-012

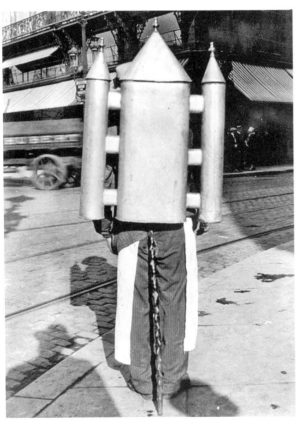
3-010

3-013

3-014

3-016

3-015

3-014. Turkey vendor in downtown street, Haiti. John W. Greene, photographer, 1940. P&P,LC-USZ62-65427.

3-015. American troops in North Africa sample the wares of a fruit vendor. Unidentified photographer, ca. 1942. P&P,FSA/OWI,LC-USW33-000797-ZC.

3-016. Chicken sellers, Mexico City, Mexico. Unidentified photographer, ca. 1912. P&P,LC-USZ62-99676.

DRIVING OR RIDING VEHICLES OR PACK ANIMALS

For bulky or large quantities of merchandise, some street vendors transport their goods in horse-drawn wagons or trucks. Others ride or lead pack animals.

3-017. Bargain day, a covered-wagon traveling salesman weighing produce, Pinehurst, North Carolina. E. L. Merrow, publisher, ca. 1900–1950. P&P,LC-USZ62-98728.

3-018. *In Washington City—1839*. Drawing by Augustus Kollner, 1839. P&P,LC-USZC4-1744.

3-017

3-018

3-019

3-020. Milk seller, Camaguey, Cuba. Unidentified photographer, ca. 1895–1920. P&P,LC-USZ62-96604.

3-020. Vegetable men, Havana, Cuba. Unidentified photographer, 1904. P&P,DETR,LC-USZ62-96624.

3-021. Milkman, Havana, Cuba. Rotograph Co., ca. 1901–1907. P&P,Postcards,PR 06(AA)CN 038,Box1(Color). LC-DIG-ppmsca-12810.

3-021

3-020

3-022

3-023

3-024

3-025

3-022. Fruit and vegetable vendor, Caracas, Venezuela. Unidentified photographer, ca. 1920–1947. P&P,AHC,Ac. No. 448. LC-DIG-ppm-sca-12472.

3-023. Goat wagon peddler, Cuba. Unidentified photographer, ca. 1895–1920. P&P,LC-USZ62-65402.

3-024. Coconut merchant's wagon, Havana, Cuba. Unidentified photographer, ca. 1890–1910. P&P,DETR,LC-D4-30877.

3-025. Fruit vendor's cart, Havana, Cuba. Unidentified photographer, 1904. P&P,DETR,LC-USZ62-96625.

3-026

3-027

3-026. Vegetable vendor, Athens, Greece. Keystone View Company, 1906. P&P,LC-USZ62-66106.

3-027. Areopagus (Mars' Hill) and Theseion, N.W. from Athens, toward Sacred Way to Eleusis. Underwood & Underwood, 1907. P&P,LC-USZ62-66122.

3-028. Vendors and a horse and cart on a street, Chinatown, San Francisco. Arnold Genthe, photographer, ca. 1896–1906. P&P,LC-G403-T-0258-B.

3-029. A Virginia vegetable cart. Unidentified photographer, ca. 1900–1910. P&P,DETR,LC-D4-33836.

3-030. Selling grapes Saturday night in the market, Boston, Massachusetts. Lewis Wickes Hine, photographer, 1909. P&P,NCLC,LC-DIG-nclc-03325.

3-028

3-029

3-030

3-031

3-031. Louis Bromberg with Nellie, Washington Wholesale Market, New York, New York. Phyllis Twachtman, photographer, 1960. P&P,NYWTS,Subj/Geog-Markets-Washington Wholesale. LC-LIG-ppmsca-12727.

A customer catches Bromberg for a purchase, just as he has finished stocking his wagon at the wholesale market.

3-032. *Watermelon man, Harlem 1940*. Aaron Siskind, photographer, 1940. P&P,PH-Siskind(A.),no.2-21(Portfolio). LC-DIG-ppmsca-12160.

3-032

SITTING AND STANDING

Most street vendors who sell from fixed locations conduct their business in streets and squares, outside public buildings and places of worship, under porticoes, or from the shelters of doorways. They place their wares on blankets spread on the ground, or they sell from baskets, portable tables, or booths.

3-033

3-033. *Progress of Reform!!! No. 1*, Lithograph with watercolor. James Baillee (New York), publisher, 1844. P&P,USZ62-12714.

Not all street vendors were welcomed. This political cartoon represents street vendors selling apples, cigars, and possibly cider, outside the gates of New York's City Hall. Two men order them to clear the sidewalk for the approaching genteel couple.

3-034

3-035

3-036

3-037

3-034. Lower water-carrier, Syr-Daria region. Man seated with urn and cup. Photoprint by N. V. Bogaevskii, 1872. From *Turkestanskii al'bom, chast' etnograficheskaia, 1871–1872*, vol. 2, part 2, p. 126. P&P,LC-USZ62-82720.

3-035. Man selling flat cakes sprinkled with sesame seeds, Turkistan. Photoprint by N. V. Bogaevskii, 1872. From *Turkestanskii al'bom, chast' promyslovaia, 1871–1872*, vol. 3, p. 37. P&P,LC-USZ62-82680.

3-036. Seller of pastries (pirozhi), Zaravshansky District, Turkistan. Photoprint by N. V. Bogaevskii, 1872. From *Turkestanskii al'bom, chast' etnograficheskaia, 1871–1872*, vol. 2, part 2, p. 144. P&P,LC-USZ62-82722.

3-037. Flat bread vendor, Samarkand. Sergei Mikhailovich Prokudin-Gorskii, photographer, ca. 1905–1915. P&P,Prok,LC-DIG-prok-11765(color).

3-038. Flat bread vendors, Samarkand. Sergei Mikhailovich Prokudin-Gorskii, photographer, ca. 1905–1915. P&P,Prok,LC-DIG-prok-02306.

3-039. Meatball vendor. American Colony (Jerusalem), Photo Department, ca. 1900–1920. P&P,LC-DIG-matpc-01249.

3-040. Pilgrims buying food from peddlers outside the Church of the Holy Sepulchre, where they are attending Easter services, Jerusalem. Underwood & Underwood, 1913. P&P,LC-DIG-ppmsca-04990.

3-039

3-038

3-040

3-041

3-041. Street fakir and some of his customers, St. Petersburg, Russia. Unidentified photographer, ca. 1902–1917. P&P,LC-USZ62-67321.

3-042. Market, Mexico(?). Unidentified photographer, before 1953. P&P,SSF:Markets Mexico 19-XXX. LC-DIG-ppmsca-12319.

3-043. *Taxco Market*, Mexico. Aquatint and etching. Howard Norton Cook, artist, 1933. P&P,LC-USZC4-1176.

3-042

3-043

3-044

3-046

3-044. *Market Scene*. Print by Maurice Prendergast, ca. 1899–1901. P&P,LC-USZC4-1784(color).

3-045. Sweet vendors, Kingston, Jamaica. C. H. Graves (The Universal Photo Art Company), stereographer, 1899. P&P,LC-USZ62-65561.

3-046. Market, Kingston, Jamaica. Lucien Wulsin, photographer, 1907. P&P,LC-USZ62-65498.

3-045

3-047. Old African American man selling strawberries on street, Washington, D.C. Frances Benjamin Johnston, photographer, ca. 1900. P&P,LC-USZ62-59598.

3-048. Stale bread vendor, Mulberry Bend, New York City, New York. Jacob A. Riis, photographer, ca. 1890. P&P,LC-USZ62-72472.

3-047

3-048

3-049

3-050

3-049. Immigrant and pretzel vendor, New York, New York. Elizabeth Alice Austen, photographer, 1896. P&P,LC-USZ62-76960.

3-050. The lily vendor, Chinatown, San Francisco, California. Arnold Genthe, photographer, ca. 1896–1906. P&P,LC-G403-T01-0363.

3-051. Lena Lochiavo, basket seller, Sixth Street Market, Cincinnati, Ohio. Lewis Wickes Hine, photographer, 1908. P&P,NCLC,LC-DIG-nclc-03200.

3-052. A foggy morning, Piccadilly Circus, London, England. Universal Photo Company, 1904. P&P,LC-USZ62-54880.

3-053. Antoinette Siminger, basket seller, Sixth Street Market, Cincinnati, Ohio. Lewis Wickes Hine, photographer, 1908. P&P,NCLC,LC-DIG-nclc-03198.

3-052

3-051

3-053

3-054

3-055

3-054. Marie Costa, basket seller, Sixth
Street Market, Cincinnati, Ohio. Lewis
Wickes Hine, photographer, 1908.
P&P,NCLC,LC-DIG-nclc-03196.

3-055. Street vendors—two men and two
boys on sidewalk with basket, New Orleans,
Louisiana. Arnold Genthe, photographer.
P&P,LC-USZ62-77239.

3-056. A peanut and candy vendor, Beijing, China. White Brothers, 1931. P&P, LC-USZ62-96763.

3-057. Market, Sumatra. Unidentified photographer. P&P, SSF:Markets-Sumatra. LC-DIG-ppmsca-12320.

3-058. Vegetable vendors, Bridgetown, Barbados. Unidentified photographer, ca. 1940. P&P, LC-USZ62-95091.

3-056

3-057

3-058

PUSHING CARTS

Some street vendors push their goods in wheeled vehicles that can be propped along the sidewalk. Pushcarts accommodate large quantities of merchandise, equipment, and supplies without the need for draft animals. They can be stowed away in nearby cellars and garages.

3-059

3-059. Japan: traveling basket vendor—man with cart full of baskets. Unidentified photographer, ca. 1915–1925. P&P,LC-USZ62-91887.

opposite:

3-060. Vendor and cart near the White House, Washington, D.C. Frances Benjamin Johnston, photographer, 1898. P&P,LC-USZ62-94133.

3-061. Peanut vendor at entrance to White House, Washington, D.C. Theodor Horydczak, photographer, ca. 1920–1950. P&P,LC-H823-2227-003.

3-062. Waffle vendor near U.S. Treasury, Washington, D.C. Unidentified photographer, ca. 1885–1895. P&P,LC-USZ6-662.

3-063. Peanut vendor, Washington, D.C. Theodor Horydczak, photographer, ca. 1920–1950. P&P,LC-H823-2227-002.

3-060

3-062

3-061

3-063

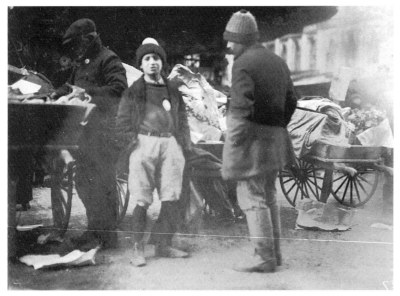

3-064

3-067

3-065

3-066

3-064. Young vendor wearing a badge at a market in Boston, Massachusetts. Lewis Wickes Hine, photographer, 1917. P&P,LC-DIG-nclc-03997.

3-065. Fruit and poultry vendor, Havana, Cuba. Unidentified photographer, ca. 1900–1906. P&P,DETR,LC-D418-9215.

3-066. Ice cream vendor, Havana, Cuba. Unidentified photographer, ca. 1890–1910. P&P,DETR,LC-D4-30879.

3-067. Peanut vendor outside the White House, Washington, D.C. Edwin Rosskam, photographer, 1940. P&P,FSA/OWI,LC-USF34-015828-E.

The area around the White House had a long history of street vending, dating back to the city's founding in 1790. This vendor is parked on Pennsylvania Avenue in between the White House (not shown) and the Treasury Building (at left)—an area now off-limits to vehicular traffic.

3-068. Italian fruit vendors, Indianapolis, Indiana. Lewis Wickes Hine, photographer, 1908. P&P,NCLC,LC-DIG-nclc-03217.

3-069. Italian street vendors with cart of dried fruit and nuts, New York, New York. Unidentified photographer, 1908. P&P,LC-B2-80-2.

3-070. Joseph Severio, peanut vendor, Wilmington, Delaware. Lewis Wickes Hine, photographer, 1910. P&P,NCLC,LC-DIG-nclc-03564(color).

3-069

3-068

3-070

3-071

3-073

3-074

3-072

3-071. Broad Street lunch carts, New York, New York. Unidentified photographer, 1906. P&P,DETR,LC-D401-19577.

3-072. Peddlers—iced drinks and snacks—August 7, 1908, New York, New York. Unidentified photographer, 1908. P&P,LC-USZ62-70752.

3-073. Clam seller in Mulberry Bend, New York, New York. Byron photographic firm, ca. 1900. P&P,DETR,LC-D401-13642.

3-074. Washington Market, New York City, New York. Arthur Rothstein, photographer, 1939. P&P,FSA/OWI,LC-USF34-027126-D.

3-075. The nut man, corner of Worth and Center streets, New York, New York. Fred Palumbo, photographer, 1947. P&P,NYWTS,Subj/Geog-Pitchmen. LC-DIG-ppmsca-12735. Fred Palumbo, photographer.

3-076. Street vendor, Warsaw, Poland. John Vachon, photographer, 1956. P&P,Look Job 56-6642-H1. LC-DIG-ppmsca-12339.

3-077. Street vendors, Warsaw, Poland. John Vachon, photographer, 1956. P&P,Look Job 56-6642-G1. LC-DIG-ppmsca-12338.

3-078. Street vendor, Rio de Janeiro, Brazil. Claudia Andujar, photographer, 1962. P&P,Look,LC-L9-62-1114-X,frame 36. LC-DIG-ppmsca-12354.

3-076

3-075

3-077

3-078

MARKETS IN PUBLIC BUILDINGS

The partnership between local government and vendors of fresh food is embodied in the mixed-use market and town hall—a combination that has its precedent in medieval Europe. This form is characterized by a single building with an open arcade on the ground floor for sheltering the trading area and a single, enclosed multipurpose room above. It is situated in the center of a public space and forms part of the larger market square.

The combined market and town hall not only provides shelter for vendors but also minimizes street disorder. By centralizing the sale of perishables (particularly fresh meat), on the ground floor of its government building, the town eliminates the need for tables and stalls in the streets. Likewise, the proximity of trade to the local authority facilitates the enforcement of weights and measures, inspection, the collection of tolls and other market fees, and the general maintenance and good order of the market. Government also enjoys a financial benefit from its physical partnership with the market, by using market revenues to finance construction and maintenance of its own quarters—be it a city hall, courthouse, or municipal building.

The mixed-use market house remained fairly constant in form over the centuries, while the function of the upper stories changed according to local need. Nineteenth-century town council minutes in the United States, for example, record dozens of multiple-use buildings with ground floor markets, including but not limited to courthouses, city council chambers, clerk's offices, fire houses, prisons, watch houses, police headquarters, armories, museums, libraries, schools, Masonic halls, opera houses, and theaters.

Several factors led to the gradual diminution in popularity of this market type by the late nineteenth century. Urban growth rendered the ground floor of the town hall insufficient to accommodate the entire market, whose space remained limited in size. Moreover, as the requirements of civic administration became more complex, the town hall gave way to the exclusive use of governmental functions. Likewise, other institutions that occasionally combined with markets in a single building, such as fire departments, armories, and theaters, developed their own distinct building types.

4-001

4-001. Market Hall, Ross-on-Wye, England. Unidentified photographer, ca. 1890–1910. P&P,Foreign Geog File-England-Ross(color). LC-DIG-ppmsca-12296.

4-002. Market Hall, Shrewsbury, England. F. Frith & Co., ca. 1880–1910. P&P,Foreign Geog File-England-Shrewsbury. LC-DIG-ppm-sca-12297.

The market was built in 1596.

4-003. Market Hall, Minchinhampton, England. F. Frith & Co., ca. 1880–1900. P&P,Foreign Geog File-England-Minchinhampton. LC-DIG-ppmsca-12295.

4-002

4-003

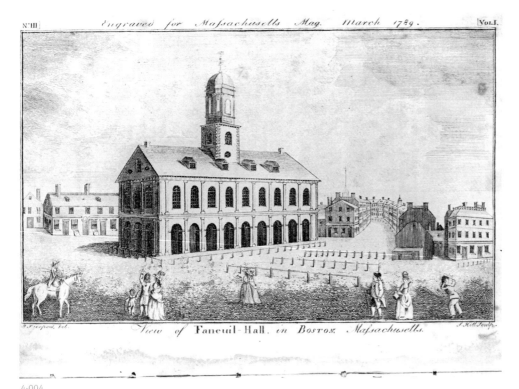

4-004

4-004. *View of Faneuil Hall in Boston, Massachusetts*. Samuel Hill, engraver, 1789. P&P,LC-USZ62-45571.

The European practice of combining town halls and markets was continued in the North American colonies. Faneuil Hall was designed by John Smibert and erected in 1740–1742 for the city of Boston.

4-005. Faneuil Hall, Boston, Massachusetts. Unidentified photographer, ca. 1890–1906. P&P,DETR,LC-D4-18829.

In 1805 Charles Bulfinch (1763–1844) added a third story and doubled the original 40-foot width.

4-005

4-006

4-007

4-007. View of south facade from southwest, Brick Market, Newport, Rhode Island. Jack E. Boucher, photographer, 1971. P&P,HABS,RI,3-NEWP,26-2.

The Brick Market, designed by Peter Harrison (1716–1775), was built in 1761–1762. It was restored by the Brick Market Foundation and now houses the Museum of Newport History.

4-008. Market House, Providence, Rhode Island. Joseph Brown and Stephen Hopkins, architects, 1773. Unidentified photographer, 1848. P&P,HABS,RI,4-PROV,42-2.

4-009. Roof being removed, Market House, Providence, Rhode Island. Unidentified photographer, 1938. P&P,HABS,RI,4-PROV,42-8.

The roof was rebuilt in 1938 after the wood trusses collapsed.

4-008

4-009

4-010. Fire Station & Municipal Offices, Winnsboro, South Carolina. Fred D. Nichols, photographer, 1940. P&P,HABS,SC,20-WINBO,1-1.

Winnsboro's town clock was originally constructed as the public market in 1833–1834. It was subsequently used as a fire station and municipal offices.

4-011. Market House, Providence, Rhode Island. George J. Vaillancourt, photographer, 1941. P&P,HABS,RI,4-PROV,42-6.

In 1950 the building was converted to academic use by the Rhode Island School of Design, which still uses it today.

4-012. Public Market Building, Oswego, New York. Design Photographics, 1967. P&P,HABS,NY,38-OSWE,1-2.

4-011

4-012

4-010

4-013

4-014

4-015

4-013. Town Hall and Market, Cheraw, South Carolina. C. O. Greene, photographer, 1940. P&P,HABS,SC,13-CHERA,2-1.

4-014. Old Market House, Galena, Illinois. Harold Huff, photographer, 1936. P&P,HABS,ILL,43-GALA,10-1.

In 1845 the City of Galena awarded the building contract to Henry J. Stouffer. The market is constructed of local Galena limestone and local red sand molded brick, with a white pine shingled roof. The stalls were on the ground floor, and the city council chamber was on the floor above. The cellar originally housed the town jail.

4-015. Old Market House, Galena, Illinois. Robert Rider Tufts, photographer, 1935. P&P,HABS,ILL,43-GALA,10-6.

4-016. Market Building, Georgetown, South Carolina. Jack E. Boucher, photographer, 1958. P&P,HABS,SC,22-GEOTO,3-1.

The Greek Revival market and town hall were built in 1842, and the clock tower and belfry were added in 1845. The Rice Museum opened in this building during the South Carolina Tricentennial in 1970. The archway behind the clock tower is still open as a public passageway.

4-016

4-017. Old Market House, Fayetteville, North Carolina. Archie A. Biggs, photographer, 1937. P&P,HABS,NC,26-FAYVI,1-3. LC-DIG-ppmsca-12809.

The combined market and town hall was built in 1838 on the site of Convention Hall, the North Carolina State House. The ground floor arcade, where produce was traded, has alternating round and pointed aches, and balustrades encircle the terraces of the two wings. The central building is embellished with Ionic pilasters on the second story and a square clock cupola. It now serves as an anchor for the historic district of Fayetteville and as the site of the city's annual dogwood festival.

4-018. "Ye Olde Market, Fayetteville, N.C." Unidentified photographer, 1946. P&P,Postcards,PR 06 (AA) CN 038, Box 4(color). LC-DIG-ppmsca-12809.

4-017

4-018

4-019

4-019. Old Market House, Fayetteville, North Carolina. Jack Delano, photographer, 1941. P&P,FSA/OWI,LC-USF34-043279-D.

4-020. Market House, Hermann, Missouri. Photocopy of illustration from William G. Bek, *The German Settlement Society of Philadelphia and Its Colony Hermann, Missouri*, (Philadelphia, PA: Americana Germanica Press, 1907). P&P,HABS,MO,37-HERM,18-1.

The market (demolished) was built in 1854–1855.

4-020

4-021

4-021. General front view, Southern Market and Municipal Building,
Mobile, Alabama. W. N. Manning, photographer, 1934.
P&P,HABS,ALA,49-MOBI,4-1.

In 1856 the city of Mobile erected a combined market and municipal
building, designed by Thomas S. James, on the east side of Royal
Street, between Government and Church. The building originally was
intended as a one-story market house that would replace the old one.
After realizing that the City Hall building had deteriorated beyond the
point of reasonable repair, the local building committee decided to add
a second story to the new market to house municipal offices.

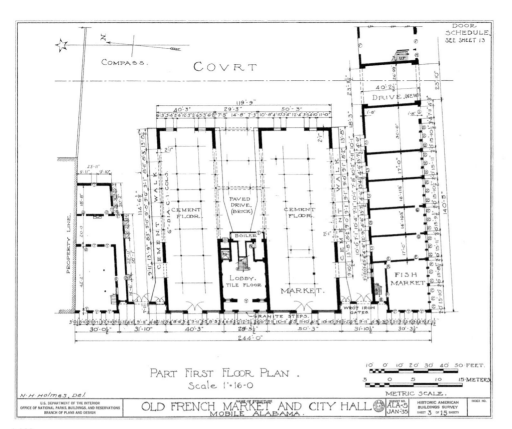

4-022

4-022. Part First Floor Plan, Southern Market and Municipal Building, Mobile, Alabama. N. H. Holmes, delineator, 1935. P&P,HABS,ALA,49-MOBI,4-,sheet no. 3.

The ground floor contained open market stands in the large courtyard and interior stalls in the south wing that faced Church Street.

4-023. Part Second Floor Plan, Southern Market and Municipal Building, Mobile, Alabama. Kenneth Engwall, delineator, 1935. P&P,HABS,ALA,49-MOBI,4-,sheet no. 5.

The municipal offices extended across the entire second story of the two main buildings, with a courtroom forming a bridge over the entrance to the market.

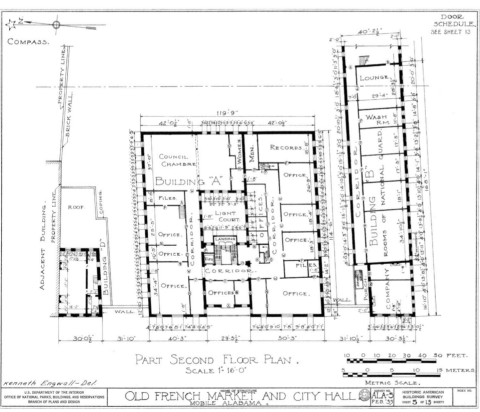

4-023

4-024. Detail of wrought-iron gates, Royal Street facade, Southern Market and Municipal Building, Mobile, Alabama. E. W. Russell, photographer, 1935. P&P,HABS,ALA,49-MOBI,4-3.

The New York Wire Railing Company furnished the iron wire for the arcades.

4-025. Courtyard view toward the west, Southern Market and Municipal Building, Mobile, Alabama. E. W. Russell, photographer, 1935. P&P,HABS,ALA,49-MOBI,4-12.

4-026. North and east fronts, overall, looking southeast, Market House and City Hall, Alexandria, Virginia. Jet Lowe, photographer, 1981. P&P,HABS,VA,7-ALEX,171-3.

German-born architect Adolf Cluss (1825–1905) designed the Alexandria City Hall and Market House in 1871. Built primarily in the Second Empire style, the building originally was U-shaped around a central courtyard. The west wing, dominated by the central clock tower, contained the city council chambers and offices on the upper level, with market stalls on the ground floor. The other wings contained an engine house, police headquarters, courthouse, Masonic temple, rental space, and other city offices. The courthouse section may have been used for additional market stalls, and there were also market sheds in the courtyard of the complex.

Benjamin F. Price was the contractor and builder for most of the details for the market section of the Alexandria City Hall, including the central clock tower, entrance doors, and butcher and huckster stalls. Cluss's contribution to the market's interior is primarily evident in the layout and arrangement of stalls, aisles, and doorways. Each stall was provided with a locked closet beneath the counter, but the marble tables, other furniture and fixtures, and ornamentation were the responsibility of the vendor. Cluss also designed Eastern Market (see 6-036) and Center Market (see 7-020), both in Washington, D.C.

4-024

4-025

4-026

4-027. West front entrance, with bell/clock tower, looking east, Market House and City Hall, Alexandria, Virginia. Jet Lowe, photographer, 1981. P&P,HABS,VA,7-ALEX,171-1.

4-028. City Hall, Laredo, Texas. Unidentified photographer, ca. 1920–1930. P&P,SSF:Markets-Texas-Laredo. LC-DIG-ppmsca-12321.

The City Hall was built in 1883–1884. The rear portion of the building, known as El Mercado, housed stalls for market vendors. Extant.

OTHER BUILDINGS WITH GROUND FLOOR MARKETS

In the late nineteenth and early twentieth centuries, cities and towns adapted the form of the combined town hall and market to new public building types, such as armories, public meeting halls, and auditoriums. Once again, the ground floor was used for marketing and the upper floor(s) served other public functions. The market was revenue producing and served to justify the cost of construction.

4-029. Market House, Meadville, Pennsylvania. Keystone View Company, publisher, 1925. P&P,LC-USZ62-93775.

The market was built in 1870 and still operates as a market and public meeting space.

4-029

SEVENTH REGIMENT ARMORY.

4-030

4-030. *Tompkins Market Armory, New York, New York.* From *New York Infantry, Seventh Regiment,* The Manual of the Seventh Regiment, National Guard, S.N.Y. (1868). Gen. Coll.,UA364 7th.A2. LC-DIG-ppmsca-12642.

The building was designed by Bogardus and Lefferts and constructed in 1857–1860. Theodore Hunt was the builder. The market occupied the ground floor, and the Armory was housed on the second and third floors. It was one of the largest cast-iron buildings in New York City.

4-031. Tompkins Market Armory, New York, New York. C. W. Woodward, stereographer, ca. 1870s. P&P,LC-USZ62-68517.

The building is labeled "Manhattan Market" on the stereograph.

4-031

4-032

4-033

4-034

4-032. Fish market, or *pescheria*, Venice, Italy. From *Builder* 108 (April 30, 1915): 406. Gen. Coll.,NA1.B5. LC-DIG-ppmsca-12680.

The covered arcade on the side of the fish market was used for retail sales. The stairway led to an upper-floor grain market.

4-033. Fish market, or *pescheria*, Venice, Italy. From *Builder* 108, (April 30, 1915): 405.Gen. Coll.,NA1.B5. LC-DIG-ppmsca-12665.

The municipality of Venice hired Cesare Laurenti and Domenico Rupolo to convert a former palazzo into a fish market. Completed in 1905, the market evokes the Byzantine Gothic style, in keeping with the traditional character of Venetian architecture. The ground floor was opened on all sides and reserved for the wholesale fish trade. The upper floor was rebuilt into a grain market, which opens onto a loggia overlooking the Grande Canal. The influence of the arts and crafts movement is evident in the detailing. The roof of the loggia comprises wooden rafters from which hangs a wrought-iron lantern designed by Laurenti. He also designed the stone capitals supporting the loggia and the fish market below with different fish and sea birds, as well as the faces of fishermen and fishwives. The market is still in use.

4-034. *The fishmarket, Venice*. Drypoint. Sir Muirhead Bone, artist, 1915. P&P,LC-USZ62-112508.

MARKET SHEDS

The simple, freestanding shed is the most prolific type of covered market. The term "shed" is used broadly to encompass the entire repertoire of structures that are usually rectilinear, supported by posts, piers, or columns, open on one or more sides, and covered by a low-pitched roof (5-008). Some market sheds are ornamented with a head house (5-018, 5-027) or false facade (5-070). Others have projecting eaves or multiple bays, in order to increase the amount of selling space or to cover large areas. A common form is the three-bay shed, with side aisles for stalls and a wider central aisle for the public concourse. This form, sometimes referred to as the basilica type, offers lighting and ventilation by means of a clerestory and was a prototype for the fully enclosed market house (5-057).

Sheds provide minimal protection from the elements for the least cost, they are quick to build relative to more substantial structures, and they do not necessarily require an architect. Builders of similar structures, such as barns and churches, are already familiar with construction techniques that employ a modular bay system to achieve the desired building length. Other advantages are its multiple entrances, which make it attractive and accessible to patrons. The open form also facilitates air circulation, the unloading of goods, and trash removal and floor cleaning at the end of the market day.

Sometimes market sheds were built over time as a string of separate structures, which allowed for cross traffic and separated the buildings by food type (5-020). They were located either in the middle of an extra-wide street to allow for traffic on both sides, or in the market square (5-010). These locations were cost-effective, since the land was already publicly owned. Usually the street of choice was not only wider but also oriented along a prominent north-south or east-west axis of a grid plan for the convenience of farmers bringing goods to market.

Market sheds have their roots in the colonnades of antiquity, such as the stoa (a portico with a wall on one side and columns or pillars on another) and arcade (covered walkway or passage having an arched roof). Over the centuries, architects and civic authorities have sought inspiration from these classical forms (5-022, 5-023, 5-067). Tents and other vernacular, open-sided structures have also inspired the development of pavilions for market sheds (5-066). These umbrella-like forms continue to inspire new designs for open market structures (5-079).

5-001

5-001. Market hall, fifteenth century, Touques (Calvados), France. From Ralph Adams Cram, *Farm Houses, Manor Houses, Minor Chateaux and Small Churches from the Eleventh to the Sixteenth Centuries in Normandy, Brittany and Other Parts of France* (1917), p. 12. Gen. Coll., NA1041.F3. LC-DIG-ppmsca-12646.

5-002. Market hall (at left), Moret-sur-Loing (Seine-et-Marne), France. Unidentified photographer, ca. 1880–1910. P&P,Foreign Geog File,France-Moret-sur-Loing(Seine-et-Marne). LC-DIG-ppmsca-12303.

5-003. *Market Hall, St. Anthème, France.* Watercolor. Cass Gilbert, artist, 1880. P&P,ADE11-Gilbert,no.264(A size)(color). LC-DIG-ppmsca-12150.

5-002

5-003

5-004

5-005

FIRST MARKET HOUSE, 1812. (STONE.)
[Drawn under direction of Fred. L. Billon.]

5-006

5-004. Market, Public Square, Louisville, Jefferson County, Georgia. Branan Sanders, photographer, 1934. P&P,HABS,GA,82-LOUVI,1-2.

The produce market was built in 1758 on what was then the site of an Indian trading post at the junction of the Georgetown and Savannah trails. The form is basically an open pavilion, made of hewn timbers, with a pitched roof capped by a belfry. Since slave traders occasionally conducted sales at this site, the building is sometimes referred to as the "slave market."

5-005. Roof plans, Market, Louisville, Georgia. Cyril B. Smith, delineator, 1934. P&P,HABS,GA,82-LOUVI,1-,sheet no. 1.

5-006. Old Market House, 1812 (Stone). From Frederick L. Billon, *Annals of St. Louis in Its Territorial Days, from 1804 to 1821* (1888), p. 25. Gen. Coll.,F474.52 B58.

5-007. *The Fish Market.* Lambert Antoine Claessens, engraver, ca. 1800–1850.P&P,LC USZ62-99159. LC-DIG-ppmsca-12663.

5-007

5-008

5-008. Public market, St. Augustine, Florida.
Prime A. Beaudoin, photographer, 1961.
P&P,HABS,FLA,55-SAUG,20-2.

The market is free-standing, with plastered
coquina (local shellstone) piers and a gable
roof. The bell tower is wooden frame construction, with slate siding and louvered
openings. The structure was built for the
sale of meat and other produce. According
to HABS documentation, it was nicknamed
the "slave market" by a photographer who
evidently labeled his views of the market as
such, presumably to boost sales of his photographs to curiosity-seeking tourists after
the Civil War.

5-009

5-009. Public market, St. Augustine, Florida. William Henry Jackson, photographer, ca. 1880–1897. P&P,DETR,LC-D418-7940.

5-010. Plaza and public market, St. Augustine, Florida. George Barker, photographer, 1886. P&P,LC-USZ62-110852.

5-011. Public market, St. Augustine, Florida, ca. 1900–1915. P&P,DETR,LC-D4-500163.

5-010

5-011

5-012

5-013

5-012. *High Street Market, Philadelphia*. William Birch & Son, engravers, 1800. P&P,LC-USZC4-548(color).

5-013. *Market Street, Albany, New York, in 1805*. P&P,Postcards,PR06(AA)CN038,Box-1. LC-DIG-ppmsca-12808.

The market shed is in the distance.

5-014. *A View of the New Market from the Corner of Shippen & Second-Streets Philada*. James Thackara, engraver, 1787. P&P,LC-USZ62-46026.

5-015. *High Street, From the Country Market-place, Philadelphia*. Hand-colored engraving by William Birch & Son, 1800. P&P,LC-USZC4-549(color).

A View of the New Market from the Corner of Shippen & Second-Streets Philada.

5-014

5-015

5-016

5-017

5-016. *New Market, in South Second Street, Philadelphia*. William Birch & Son, engravers, 1800. P&P,LC-USZC4-555(color).

5-017. *Second Street Market, Philadelphia*. Etching by Joseph Pennell, 1920. P&P,FP-XIX-P420,no.748-I(Asize). LC-DIG-ppmsca-12162.

5-018. Second Street Market, Philadelphia, Pennsylvania. Jack E. Boucher, photographer, 1963. P&P,HABS,PA,51-PHILA,28-2.

The head house served as the quarters for the Hope Hose Company No. 6 & Fellowship Engine Company. The building was listed on the National Register of Historic Places in 1966.

5-018

5-019. South Second Street Market, Philadelphia, Pennsylvania. Ph. B. Wallace, photographer, 1933. P&P,LC-USZ62-111513.

5-020. Map of South Second Street Market, Philadelphia, Pennsylvania. From *Insurance Maps of the City of Philadelphia* (Philadelphia, PA: Ernest Hexamer & Son, 1895), plate 3. G&M,G1264. P5H,v.1,1895–1898 fol.,(color),detail.

Identified in this map are the many commercial establishments that typically surrounded the market's two rows of sheds—in this case, a bank, hotel, restaurant, bakery, confectioner, barber shop, photographer, tin shop, cigar manufacturer, upholsterer, carpet weaver, Chinese laundry, hatter, muslin underwear dealer, shoe shop, and scale company.

5-019

5-020

5-021

5-022

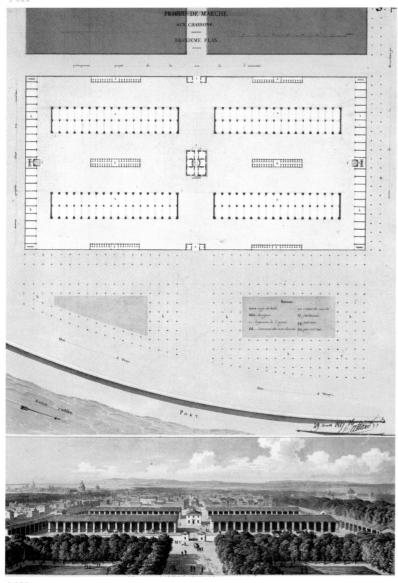

5-023

5-024

5-021. *The Germantown Market Place, now Market Square, Philadelphia, Pennsylvania.* Unidentified photographer, 1905. P&P,LC-USZ62-96612.

5-022. Meat Market, New Orleans, Louisiana. From I. Tanesse, *Plan of the City and Suburbs of New Orleans* (1815). G&M,G4014 N5 1815.T3, detail.

5-023. *Projet de Marché aux Charbons [Paris]. Deuxième Plan.* Louis-Pierre Baltard, architect. Watercolor, 1817. P&P,DLC/PP2000:029.6(color). LC-DIG-ppmsca-12814.

Louis-Pierre Baltard, father of Victor Baltard (1764–1846), architect of Les Halles, prepared plans for a market that specialized in the sale of mineral coal from the north of France. The walled complex encircled two sets of parallel sheds with an administrative building in the center. The site also contained offices for merchants along the perimeter, as well as latrines and warehouses. The sale of other bulky goods that arrived in the French capital principally by water, such as grain, wood, charcoal, and oysters, was conducted in similar markets along the quays of the Seine before the expansion of the railway system. Baltard's proposed coal market was situated at the westernmost side of the Quai d'Orsay, on the foundations of the former Palais des Archives, and faced across the Seine toward Chaillot.

5-024. Theater and hotel building, Richmond, Virginia. Drawing by Benjamin Henry Latrobe, architect, 1797 or 1798. P&P,ADE-Unit 2885,no.8(Csize). LC-USZ62-22881.

The Shockoe Hill Market is the arcaded building on the right.

5-025. *2e Projet de Marché aux Charbons [Paris]*. Louis-Pierre Baltard, architect. Watercolor, 1817. P&P,DLC/PP 2000:029,(?)(color). LC-DIG-ppmsca-12813.

The masonry sheds were two bays wide by seventeen bays long and featured an early adaptation of iron to the roof framing. Prior to this time, most French markets were constructed of masonry with very large arched openings and with heavy, timber-framed roofs.

5-026. Market, Cochabamba, Bolivia. Unidentified photographer, ca. 1920–1947. P&P,AHC,Ac. No. 831.

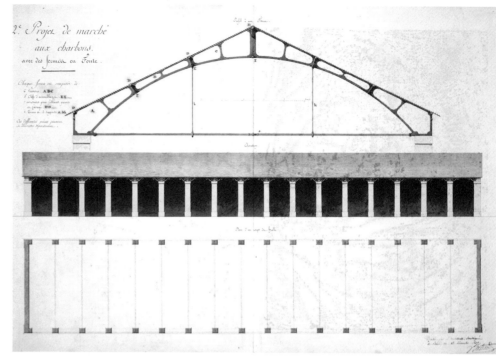

5-025

5-026

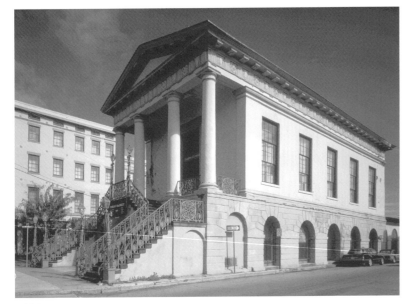

5-027

5-027. Market Hall, Charleston, South Carolina. Gilford Photography, 1985. P&P,HABS,SC,10-CHAR,6-76(color).

The market hall, designed by Edward Brickell White (1806–1882), has been the centerpiece of the city since 1841. In 1992 the City of Charleston began restoration of the building, which had sustained heavy damage during Hurricane Hugo. The goal of the project was to conserve the original building fabric and to use traditional methods and materials to repair or replace missing sections. After a ten-year-long effort, the award-winning $3 million restoration project was completed. The open ground floor provides space for market vendors, and the top floor has reopened as a museum and meeting hall. The stucco walls of Market Hall are now painted in their original color—ochre—instead of the more familiar whitewash; and the wrought-iron railings, once painted black, are now light green. Market Hall still serves as the grand entrance to the row of market sheds that stretch for several blocks toward the Cooper River.

5-028. Perspective view of west (front) and north side showing roof, Market Hall, Charleston, South Carolina. John McWilliams, photographer, 1990. P&P,HABS,SC,10-CHAR,6-27.

5-029. Market Hall, Charleston, South Carolina. Unidentified photographer, 1865. P&P,LC-DIG-cwpb-03010.

5-028

5-029

5-030. Location map, Market Hall, Charleston, South Carolina. Robert C. Giebner, delineator, 1990. P&P,HABS,SC,10-CHAR,6-,sheet no. 1.

5-031. Ground floor entrance and grill detail, Market Hall, Charleston, South Carolina. Gilford Photography, 1985. P&P,HABS,SC,10-CHAR,6-13.

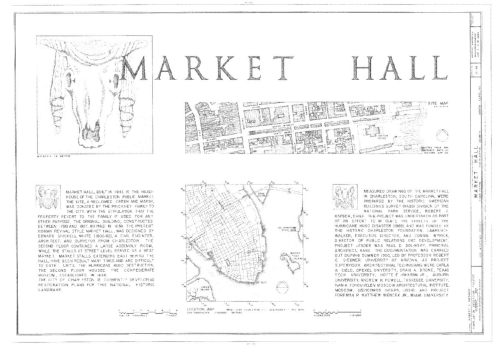

5-030

5-031

5-032

5-032. Market, Charleston, South Carolina. Unidentified photographer, 1907. P&P,DETR,LC-D423-101.

5-033. Market Hall, Shed No. 1, Charleston, South Carolina. Charles Bayless, photographer, 1978. P&P,HABS,SC,10-CHAR,6A-1.

5-034. Market Hall, Shed No. 2, Charleston, South Carolina. Charles Bayless, photographer, 1978. P&P,HABS,SC,10-CHAR,6B-1.

5-033

5-034

5-035. Market Hall, Shed No. 3, Charleston, South Carolina. Charles Bayless, photographer, 1978. P&P,HABS,SC,10-CHAR, 6C-1.

5-036. Market Hall, Shed No. 4, Charleston, South Carolina. Charles Bayless, photographer, 1978. P&P,HABS,SC,10-CHAR, 6D-1.

5-037. Market Hall, Shed No. 5, Charleston, South Carolina. Charles Bayless, photographer, 1978. P&P,HABS,SC,10-CHAR, 6E-1.

5-035

5-036

5-037

5-038

5-039

5-038. French Market, New Orleans, Louisiana. Unidentified photographer, ca. 1910. P&P,DETR,LC-D4-71846.

5-039. Market house, Savannah, Georgia. Samuel A. Cooley, photographer, 1865. P&P,LC-DIG-cwpb-03221.

This is the Congress Street facade of the pre-1870 Savannah market house, probably built in 1822.

5-040. *Market, New Orleans*. Etching. Elizabeth Lentz, artist, ca. 1944. P&P,FP-XX-L5749,n.1(Asize). LC-DIG-ppmsca-1216.

5-041. Fruit stand, New Orleans, Louisiana. Unidentified photographer, ca. 1900–1920. P&P,LC-USZ62-90735.

5-040

5-041

5-042. Market scene, New Orleans, Louisiana. Arnold Genthe, photographer, ca. 1920–1924. P&P,Genthe,LC-USZ62-112756.

5-043. Corner of the French Market, New Orleans, Louisiana. DETR, ca. 1900–1910. P&P,DETR,LC-D4-39639.

5-044. French Market, Public Works Administration, 1939. New Orleans, Louisiana. P&P, NA712 .A5 1939(Case Y). LC-DIG-ppm-sca-12641.

The Public Works Administration of the federal government completed this project in 1938. It involved alterations and additions to the existing meat market; the erection of a new building for fruit, vegetable, and poultry markets, and a restaurant; and alterations to the original market shed and coffee shop.

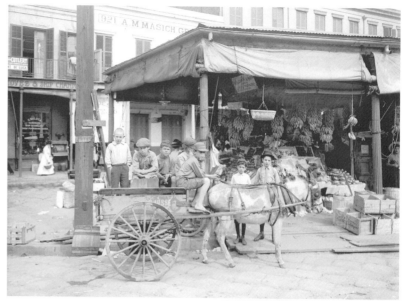

5-043

5-042

5-044

5-045

5-047

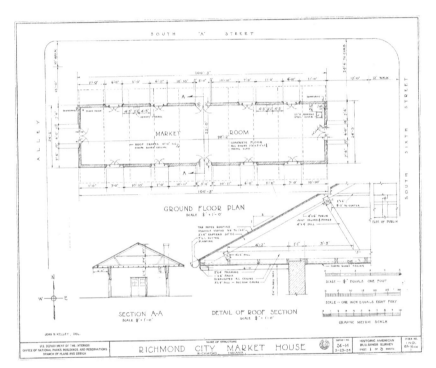

5-046

5-045. City Market House, Richmond, Indiana. John R. Kelley, photographer, 1934. P&P,HABS,IND,89-RICH,1-2.

John A. McMinn built the brick market in 1855 according to the plans of James M. Smith. The door openings have since been partially bricked up. This photograph was taken shortly after the market was painted and repaired by the Civil Works Administration.

5-046. Old market, Richmond, Virginia. Keystone View Company, 1909. P&P,LC-USZ62-79328.

5-047. Ground floor plan and sections, City Market House, Richmond, Indiana. John R. Kelley, delineator, 1934. P&P,HABS,IND,89-RICH,1-,sheet no. 1.

5-048. Site and location plan, Centre Market, Wheeling, West Virginia, Robert Meden and Kathleen Hoeft, delineators, 1974. P&P,HAER,WVA,35-WHEEL,3-,sheet no. 1.

The original 1853 market house occupies the northern half of the market square and was joined in 1890 by a second market house immediately to the south.

5-049. Isometric drawing, Centre Market, Wheeling, West Virginia. Stephen Hawks and Martin Greenberg, delineators, 1974. P&P,HAER,WVA,35-WHEEL,3-,sheet no. 2.

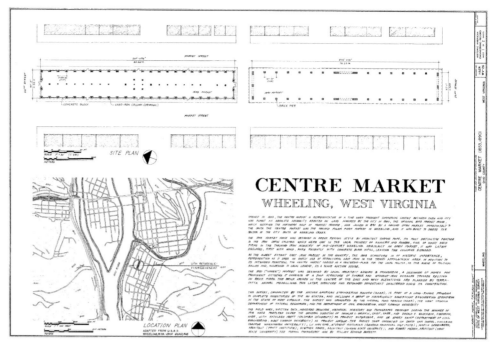

5-048

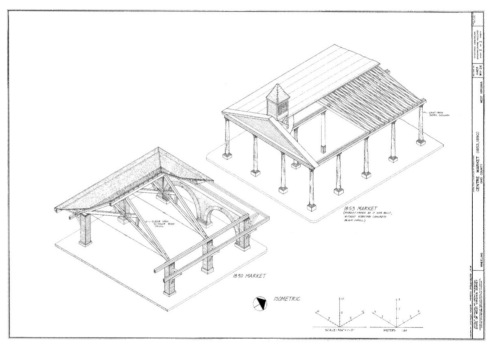

5-049

5-050

5-051

5-052

5-050. Centre Market, Wheeling, West Virginia. Jack Boucher, photographer, 1977. P&P,HAER,WVA,35-WHEEL,3-6.

The 1853 market house was designed by Thomas Pope in the neoclassical style, with three aisles divided by cast-iron Doric columns. The columns were cast by the local foundry of Hamilton and Rogers. Alternate columns serve as downspouts. The building has a gabled roof with dentilated cornice, and a belfy at the south end. Stalls were arranged in three rows: vegetables were sold on either side, and butchers sold from stalls in the center aisle. The stalls were replaced in the twentieth century with refrigerators, display cases, and folding tables, and the structure was enclosed with cinder block infill construction. In 1983 the interior still had the original pressed tin ceiling and cornice molding.

5-051. Centre Market, Wheeling, West Virginia. View of the lower market (1890). Jack Boucher, photographer, 1977. P&P,HAER,WVA,35-WHEEL,3-9.

The lower market was built in 1890. Edward B. Franzheim, a local architect trained in Boston, designed the building in the Romanesque revival style. It is open on the sides and consists of a hipped roof supported on brick piers. The market is also noted for its deep overhanging eaves, with cross gables in the center of the east and west elevations. Centre Market continues to operate as a market year-round.

5-052. Centre Market, Wheeling, West Virginia. View of the interior of the lower market (1890). Jack Boucher, photographer, 1977. P&P,HAER,WVA,35-WHEEL,3-12.

The roof—originally slate and now shingle—is supported by wooden scissor trusses.

5-053. Centre Market, Wheeling, West Virginia. Entrance to the lower market showing animal medallions flanking arch. Jack Boucher, photographer, 1977. P&P,HAER,WVA,35-WHEEL,3-13.

Terra cotta medallions of animal heads flank the arches of the cross gables.

5-054. Centre Market, Wheeling, West Virginia. Detail of boar's head to right of arch. Jack Boucher, photographer, 1977. P&P,HAER,WVA,35-WHEEL,3-15.

5-055. Centre Market, Wheeling, West Virginia. Detail of cow's head to left of arch. Jack Boucher, photographer, 1977. P&P,HAER,WVA,35-WHEEL,3-14.

5-053

5-054

5-055

THE MARKET HOUSE

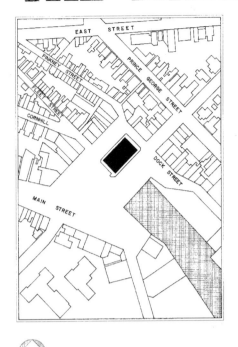

THE ANNAPOLIS MARKET HOUSE WAS CONSTRUCTED IN 1857–1858 UNDER THE SUPERINTENDENCE OF A COMMITTEE APPOINTED BY CITY COUNCIL. THE EXISTING ONE STORY BUILDING, 2 ND. MARKET TO BE ERECTED ON THIS SITE, SET ASIDE FOR THIS USE IN 1784, WAS ORIGINALLY A HIPPED-ROOFED STRUCTURE SUPPORTED BY FOUR ROWS OF CAST IRON COLUMNS. THE HIPPED SECTION AT THE NORTHERN END HAS BEEN REMOVED AND TILE BLOCK / STUCCO WALLS WITH STEEL PIVOTED WINDOWS ADDED, CLOSING IN THE OPEN SIDES AND ELIMINATING THE FOUR FOOT ROOF OVERHANG. THE SKYLIGHTED ROOF STRUCTURE IS ALSO LATER. THE ORIGINAL BRICK SCALE HOUSES STILL STAND, WITH MINOR CHANGES, AND ALL BUT FOUR OF THE ORIGINAL COLUMNS REMAIN IN PLACE.

NORTH

SCALE IN FEET
0 50 100 200

DRAWN BY RUSSELL WRIGHT MAY 1970
HISTORIC ANNAPOLIS INCORPORATED
UNDER DIRECTION OF THE NATIONAL PARK SERVICE,
UNITED STATES DEPARTMENT OF THE INTERIOR

NAME AND LOCATION OF STRUCTURE
· THE MARKET HOUSE · ANNAPOLIS, MARYLAND ·
ANNE ARUNDEL COUNTY

SURVEY NO.
MD
264
234

HISTORIC AMERICAN
BUILDINGS SURVEY
SHEET 1 OF 4 SHEETS

5-056

5-056. Site plan, Market House, Annapolis, Maryland. Russell Wright, delineator, 1970. P&P, HABS, MD, 2-ANNA, 58-, sheet no. 1.

The market still stands in its original location along the waterfront and is now under consideration for renovation or redevelopment by the city.

5-057. Lexington Market, Baltimore, Maryland. Unidentified photographer, ca. 1900–1910. P&P,DETR,LC-D4-43299.

The first shed appeared on the site in 1803, and the market was greatly expanded shortly after the Civil War. By 1925 over 1,000 stalls under three-block-long sheds constituted the market area. The sheds burned in 1949, but the market reopened in 1952. Lexington Market remains Baltimore's largest public market.

5-058. Lexington Market, Baltimore, Maryland. Unidentified photographer, 1903. P&P,DETR,LC-D401-16538.

5-059. Lexington Market, Baltimore, Maryland. Albertype Co., ca. 1900–1910. P&P,LC-USZ62-15860.

5-057

5-058

5-059

MORNING
The Market

NOON
Cleaning up.

T.W.A. Rogers.

AFTERNOON.
The Children's Playground.

COLONEL WARING'S PROPOSED EAST-SIDE PUSH-CART PEDDLERS' MARKET AND CHILDREN'S PLAY-GROUND.
DRAWN BY W. A. ROGERS.—[SEE PAGE 1237.]
1238

5-060

5-060. George Waring's proposal for a combined market and playground. From *Harper's Weekly* 39 (December 28, 1895): 1237. Gen. Coll.,AP2 .H32.

George E. Waring Jr. (1833–1898), the great sanitary engineer, proposed to the Mayor of New York a combination market and playground. The stalls would be suspended by chains from the ceiling so that they could be removed from the market floor as needed. At the beginning of the day, businesses would open for marketing. Then at noon, city street sweepers would raise the stalls to the ceiling and sweep the floor clear of debris. At the end of the day, children could use the cleared floor as a playground, until the cycle repeated.

5-061. Market, Jolo, Philippine Islands. Unidentified photographer, ca. 1900–1920. P&P,Foreign Geog File-Philippine Islands. LC-DIG-ppmsca-12312.

In 1898 the colonial administration of the Philippines was transferred from Spain to the United States. In 1905 the U.S.-ruled Department of Commerce and Police established the Bureau of Public Works and appointed William E. Parsons as Government and Architect for the Philippines—a post he held from 1905 to 1914. Parsons, who trained at the Ecole des Beaux-Arts in Paris, had general supervision over the design of all public buildings on the islands, including markets. The standard plan for provincial municipal markets was a freestanding shed with a ventilated hipped roof supported by reinforced concrete piers. The expansive floor area was concrete in order to allow for washing at the end of the day; it was void of furnishings so that food could not remain overnight. Parsons also supervised the design of fully enclosed markets (see 6-020).

5-062. Market, Kinigoran, Philippine Islands. Unidentified photographer, ca. 1900–1930. P&P,Foreign Geog File-Philippine Islands. LC-DIG-ppmsca-12944.

5-063. Market, Pampanga, Philippine Islands. Unidentified photographer, ca. 1900–1930. P&P,LC-USZ62-97356.

5-061

5-062

5-063

5-064

5-064. Market, Hogonoy, Philippine Islands. Unidentified photographer, ca. 1900–1920. P&P, Foreign Geog File-Philippine Islands.

This market was located along the natural lines of transportation.

5-065. Market, Morgan City, Louisiana. Harry L. Squires, photographer, ca. 1904. P&P, SSF. Markets-LA-Morgan City. LC-DIG-ppmsca-12323.

5-065

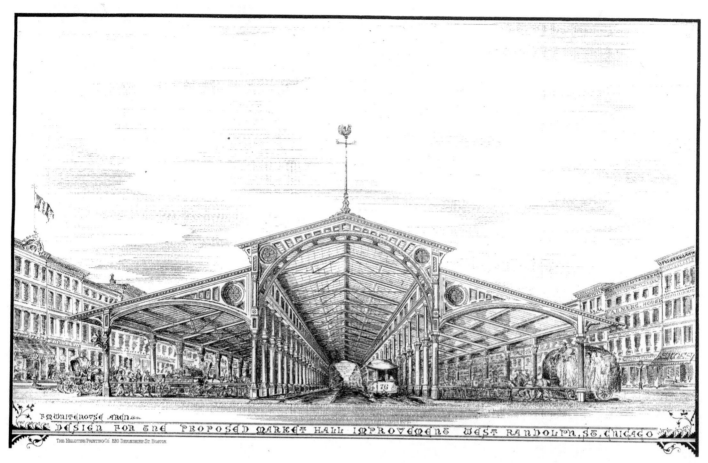

5-066

5-066. Design for the proposed market hall improvement, West Randolph Street, Chicago, Illinois. F. M. Whitehouse, architect. From *American Architect and Building News*, January 26, 1878, p. 109. Gen. Coll., NA1.A3. LC-DIG-ppmsca-12672.

The proposed iron market was designed for streetcar traffic in the central bay and open air marketing in the side aisles.

5-067. Mercato Nuovo, Florence, Italy. Sixteenth century. Unidentified photographer, ca. 1890–1910. P&P,Foreign Geog File-Italy-Florence(color). LC-DIG-ppmsca-12304.

5-067

5-068

5-069

5-070

5-068. Flower Market, Quai de la Cité, Paris. Frances Benjamin Johnston, photographer, 1925 or 1926. P&P,LC-USZ62-120442.

5-069. Municipal Market, Charlotte Amalie, St. Thomas Island, Virgin Islands. Jack Delano, photographer, 1941. P&P,FSA/OWI,LC-USF33-021391-M2.

5-070. Farmers Market, Shreveport, Louisiana. P&P,NA712.A5 1939(Case Y). LC-DIG-ppmsca-12660.

The market, constructed in 1935 by the Public Works Administration, consisted of matching steel sheds with brick false facades.

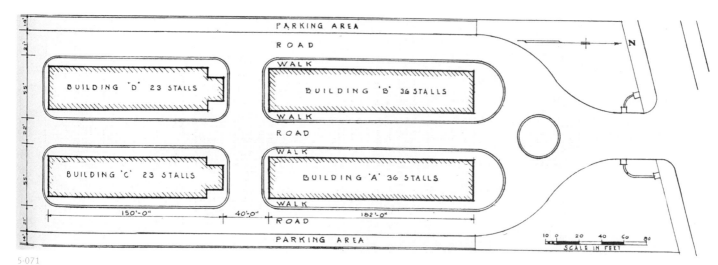

5-071

5-071. Site plan, Farmers Market, Shreveport, Louisiana. From C. W. Short and R. Stanley-Brown, *Public Buildings: A Survey of Architecture of Projects Constructed by Federal and Other Governmental Bodies between the Years 1933 and 1939* (Washington, DC: Public Works Administration, 1939), p. 629. Gen. Coll.,NA4208.A4. LC-DIG-ppmsca-12661.

5-072. Center Market, Washington, D.C. Dorothea Lange, photographer, 1936. P&P,FSA/OWI,LC-USF34-009535-C.

Given the date, this could be the Florida Avenue Market, which replaced Center Market after it was torn down in 1931.

5-073. Center Market, Washington, D.C. Dorothea Lange, photographer, 1936. P&P,FSA/OWI,LC-USF34-009538-C.

5-072

5-073

5-074

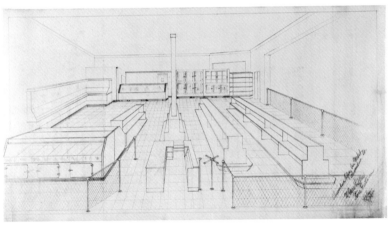

5-075

5-076

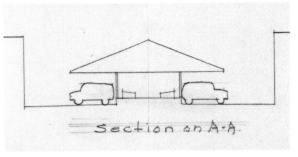

5-077

5-074. Center Market, Washington, D.C. Dorothea Lange, photographer, 1936. P&P,FSA/OWI,LC-USF34-T01-009525-C.

5-075. Architectural drawing for a market (Alexandria Open Air Market), Alexandria, Virginia. Luther R. Ray, architect, 1942. P&P,LC-USZ62-116881.

5-076. Fruit market, Benton Harbor, Michigan. John Vachon, photographer, 1940. P&P,FSA/OWI,LC-USF34-061207-D.

Growers pay ten cents to drive their truck through the market. If produce is not sold at the end of the line, it must enter through the gate again.

5-077. Elevation drawing of a shed for a farmers' market for the Alley Clearance Authority, Washington, D.C., Scheme A. Allied Architects, Inc., 1936. P&P,ADE-UNIT724,no.1(C size),detail. LC-DIG-ppmsca-12154.

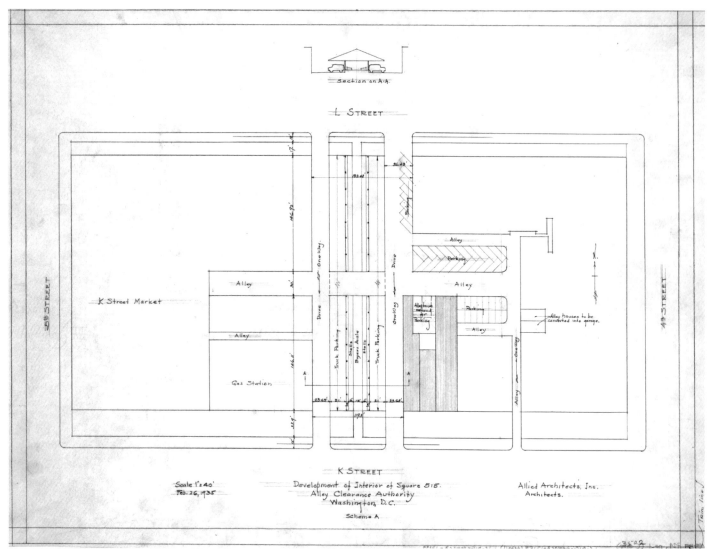

5-078. Site plan for a farmers' market for the Alley Clearance
Authority, Washington, D.C., Scheme A. Arthur B. Heaton, architect (?), Allied Architects, Inc., 1936. LC-DIG-ppmsca-12155.

5-079. Covered market, Piazza del Mercato, Pescia, Italy. Brizzi,
Gori, Gori, Ricci, and Savioli, architects. From G. E. Kidder Smith,
The New Architecture: An Illustrated Guidebook and Appraisal
(1961), no. 11, p. 174. Corbis. Gen. Coll.,NA958.S6. LC-DIG-ppm-
sca-12830.

Kidder Smith describes the market as a "soaring scalloped shell
of concrete, poised lightly on lateral supports, hover[ing] like a
great umbrella weightlessly and effortlessly over its 75-foot
span."

ENCLOSED MARKET HOUSES

During the second half of the nineteenth century, many cities and towns tore down their market sheds and replaced them with fully enclosed market houses. This movement was the result of a desire to civilize public space and to transform streets into conduits of transportation. The enclosed market house required new architectural strategies, as architects and engineers looked for ways to contain market activity without discouraging it. The most persistent type was the enclosed shed, basically rectilinear, with multiple aisles lined with stalls or booths, and a clerestory. Interior colonnades and avenues mimicked the streets and encouraged shoppers to stroll and inspect goods, without the interference of traffic and inclement weather. Developments in cast-iron architecture enabled the construction of large covered spaces unencumbered by the proliferation of internal supports.

The fully enclosed market house permitted year-round sales and justified more elaborate interior furniture and fixtures relative to the open-air shed. Butcher stalls, for example, might be equipped with marble countertops and butcher blocks.

Stalls and stands were also sized according to the type of goods, with butcher stalls typically larger than stalls devoted to the sale of produce, butter, cheese, and eggs. Farmers selling seasonal goods, such as fruits and vegetables, could not justify the cost of renting a year-round stall, so provisions were made for them to sell in designated spaces outside of the market, in the courtyard, or under a farmers' shed adjacent to the market house.

6-001

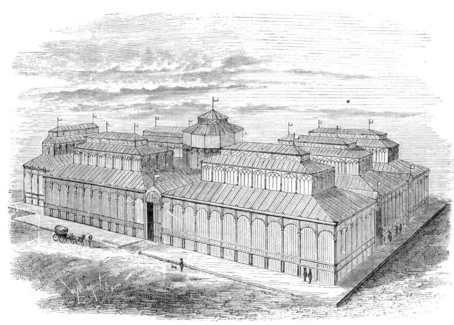

6-002

6-001. Central Market, Göteborg, Sweden. Keystone View Company, 1906. P&P,Stereographs-Sweden-Göteborg. LC-DIG-ppmsca-12325.

This market is still in operation.

6-002. Perspective drawing of E. Mathieu's design for the market in the Plaza de la Cebada, Madrid, Spain, erected in 1872–1873. From Ewing Matheson, *Works in Iron. Bridge and Roof Structures* (1877), p. 252. Gen. Coll.,TG 145 .M3. LC-DIG-ppmsca-12643.

The city replaced this structure with a new market building in 1962.

6-003. Portal of the Iron Market, Port-au-Prince, Haiti. Unidentified photographer, 1890. P&P,DETR,LC-USZ62-65400. LC-DIG-ppmsca-12643.

This elaborate market house, constructed of cast-iron and tin parts, was fabricated in France in 1886 and exported to Haiti for assembly.

6-003

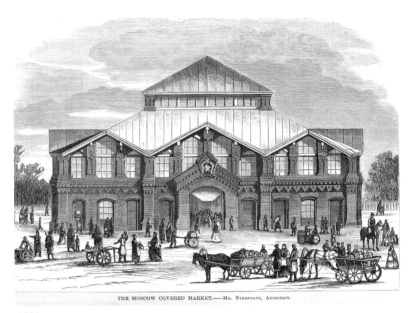

THE MOSCOW COVERED MARKET.—Mr. Nikeforvu, Architect.

6-004

6-005

market in Paris. 1880

6-006

6-004. Moscow covered market, Russia. From *Builder* 35 (1877): 532. Gen. Coll.,NA1.B5. LC-DIG-ppmsca-12664.

M. T. Nikeforvu, architect of the Town Council, designed the market house in 1876. It measured 175 by 70 feet and contained space for up to forty-eight shops. The roof was supported by iron trusses resting on twelve stone pillars. At the time of its opening, the floor was wooden, pending the installation of asphalt. The interior was lighted by gas and furnished with two spring-fed water basins. Builder noted the city's coat of arms over the main entrance, as well as the city's plan to build similar markets on four more squares.

6-005. Market Hall, Montevideo, Uruguay. Unidentified photographer, ca. 1920–1940. P&P,AHC-Architecture-Uruguay. LC-DIGppmsca-12473.

6-006. *Market in Paris*. Watercolor by Cass Gilbert, 1880. P&P,ADE11-Gilbert,no.272(A size)(color). LC-DIG-ppmsca-12151.

6-007. City market, Masaya, Nicaragua. Keystone View Company, 1902. P&P,LC-USZ62-98420.

6-008. Mercado de Tacón, Havana, Cuba. Unidentified photographer, 1904. P&P,DETR,LC-D4-17663.

The market was built in 1874–1879 and occupied the entire block bound by Galiano, Reina, Dragones, and Aguila avenues. Designed by Eugenio Rayneri y Sorrentino (1841–1922), the market was noted for its elegant facade, marked by the street-level arcade and second-story balconies that ran along the perimeter. The market was also embellished with a four-sided clock tower. Rayneri used iron in the graceful railings of the exterior balconies and for the interior supports.

6-007

6-008

6-009

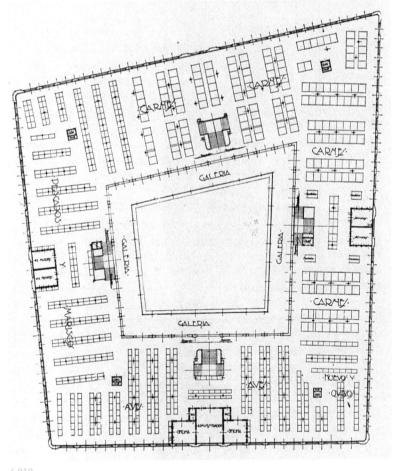

6-010

6-0011

6-009. Vegetable stands in Mercado de Tacón, Havana, Cuba. Unidentified photographer, 1904. P&P,DETR,LC-D401-17664.

6-010. Floor plan, Tryon Market, Havana, Cuba. From Arthur Goodwin, *Markets: Public and Private* (1929), p. 111. Gen. Coll., HE5470.G6. LC-DIG-ppmsca-12863.

The farmers' section of the market was located in the courtyard, which provided off-street parking for wagons.

6-011. Mercado de Tacón, Havana, Cuba. Strohmeyer & Wyman, 1899. P&P,LC-USZ62-65589.

6-012. Market, Cuba. Unidentified photographer, ca. 1895–1920. P&P,LC-USZ62-96598.

6-012

6-013

6-014

6-015

6-013. Market, Caracas, Venezuela. Unidentified photographer, ca. 1900–1906. P&P,DETR,LC-D4-9245.

6-014. Interior of food market, Zacatecas, Mexico. Charles Burlingame Waite, photographer, 1904. P&P,LC-USZ62-114768.

6-015. New public market, San Juan, Puerto Rico. Unidentified photographer, ca. 1890–1923. P&P,LC-USZ62-101305.

This photograph was probably taken just after construction. The conspicuous absence of market activity seems to suggest that the aim of this image was to boast the architectural merits of the building. The basilica-type structure, with its clerestory and high ceilings, admits ample indirect light and ventilation. The selling space has been designed with three different kinds of trade in mind—with open counters lined up in the main aisle, caged stalls probably for poultry sales, and fully enclosed shops. Also note the gallery, which permitted market officials a privileged view from which to oversee the market.

6-016. Market Square, Hamilton, Canada. Unidentified photographer, ca. 1890. P&P,Souvenir Viewbooks-Foreign-Canada-Hamilton. LC-DIG-ppmsca-12316.

6-017. Mercado Luis Terrazas, Juarez, Mexico. Unidentified photographer, 1907. P&P,DETR,LC-D4-19803.

The market was dedicated in 1905.

6-018. Bananas, coconuts, rice, beans, and other produce for sale at the produce market, Rio Piedras, Puerto Rico. Jack Delano, photographer, 1942. P&P,FSA/OWI,LC-USF34-047454-D.

6-016

6-017

6-018

6-019

6-020

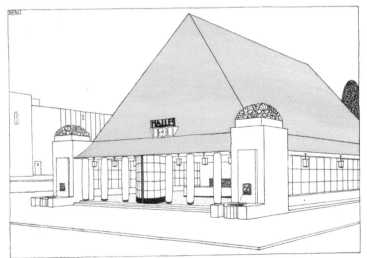
6-021

6-022

6-019. Purchasing chickens at the produce market, Rio Piedras, Puerto Rico. Jack Delano, photographer, 1942. P&P,FSA/OWI,LC-USF34-047469-D.

6-020. Municipal Market, Paco, Manila, Philippine Islands. From *Architectural Record* 41, no. 4 (1917): fig. 29. Gen. Coll.,NA1.A6. LC-DIG-ppmsca-12674.

6-021. *Halles—Market Place*. Lithograph. Robert Mallet-Stevens, architect, 1922. P&P,LC-USZC4-2586(color).

6-022. Selling barbecued pork and native pork products at the market, Rio Piedras, Puerto Rico. Jack Delano, photographer, 1942. P&P,FSA/OWI,LC-USF34-047467-D.

HALLES — MARKET PLACE

6-023

6-024

6-025

6-023. Main city market, interior, Arkhangelsk, Russia. William C. Brumfield, photographer, 1999. P&P,Brum,LC-DIG-ppmsc-02952(color).

6-024. Main city market (1980s), Arkhangelsk, Russia. William C. Brumfield, photographer, 1999. P&P,Brum,LC-DIG-ppmsc-02951(color).

6-025. Covered market, boulevard A. Briand, Royan, France. From G. E. Kidder Smith, *The New Architecture: An Illustrated Guidebook and Appraisal* (1961), no. 20, p. 110. Gen. Coll.,NA958.S6. LC-DIG-ppmsca-12831.

Simon and Morisseau, architects, and R. Sarger, engineer, chose a sinusoidal paraboloid in concrete for the central market in Royan. Thirteen paraboloids, with their distinctive undulations, form arches over the entrances around the periphery. The building is 171 feet in diameter and 34.5 feet high at the center.

EAST VIEW OF FANEUIL HALL MARKET.

Engraved for Bowen's Picture of Boston.

6-026

6-026. *East view of Faneuil Hall Market, Boston.* Abel Bowen, engraver, ca. 1810–1850. P&P,LC-USZ62-90358.

In 1823 Boston's Mayor, Josiah Quincy, launched a massive and controversial urban renewal project just east of Faneuil Hall (in partial view in the background). Quincy commissioned Alexander Parris (1780–1852) to design a new granite market house flanked by a row of standardized warehouses. The project involved the removal of narrow streets and the demolition of dilapidated buildings on land that the city obtained by eminent domain. The city constructed the domed section in the center of the market house and auctioned the surrounding lots to investors, who then built the wings in accordance with Parris's plans. Quincy Market, as it was popularly known, was a masterpiece of civic design and served as Boston's chief food distribution center for the next 125 years.

PLAN OF STALLS IN FANEUIL HALL MARKET, BOSTON.

[Entered according to Act of Congress, in the Year 1849, by GEO. K. SNOW & CO., in the Clerk's Office of the District Court of Massachusetts.]

NORTH MARKET STREET.

Length of Floor, 512 ft. Width of main Passage, 10 ft. Depth of Stalls, 17 ft. Height of do. 14 ft.

SOUTH MARKET STREET.

Geo. K. Snow &co. Propr   Dep. Aug 11. 1849.
Ser Vol. 24. P. 254.

6-027

6-028

6-029

6-027. Plan of stalls in Faneuil Hall Market, Boston, Massachusetts. George K. Snow & Company, delineator, 1849. AM,An American Time Capsule,Printed Ephemera Collection,Portfolio 59,Folder 22b.

6-028. Quincy Market and Faneuil Hall, Boston, Massachusetts. Keystone View Company, 1905. P&P,LC-USZ62-78671.

6-029. Quincy Market, the produce center, from Faneuil Hall, Boston, Massachusetts. H. C. White Company, 1906. P&P,LC-USZ62-78670.

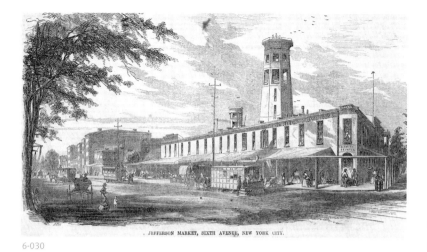

6-030

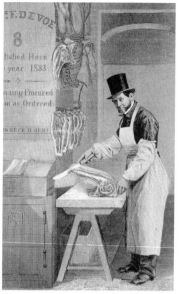

6-031

6-032

6-033

6-030. Jefferson Market, New York, New York. From *Ballou's Pictorial Drawing Room Companion*, October 17, 1857. P&P, AP2.B227. LC-DIG-ppmsca-12639.

6-031. Thomas F. DeVoe (1811–1892), butcher, Jefferson Market, New York, New York. From Thomas F. DeVoe, *The Market Assistant* (1867), frontispiece. Gen. Coll., TX353 .D48.

Following his career as a butcher, DeVoe was superintendent of the public markets for New York City in the 1870s. At the same time, he published several books and articles on the history of public markets, principally about those in New York City. DeVoe's letters and manuscripts are housed in the New-York Historical Society.

6-032. Frame wing, Broad Street Market, Harrisburg, Pennsylvania. View from the southeast. Bryson Leidich Photography, 1977. P&P, HABS, PA, 22-HARBU, 4A-1.

This frame structure, with board and batten siding, was built as an addition to the existing stone market building (built 1856–1860) in the background. Also part of the market complex is a brick market house (built 1874–1886) located to the right of the picture frame (not shown). The frame addition was demolished in 1977, but the stone and brick market buildings still stand. The Broad Street Market has been in continuous operation since the 1860s and is on the National Register of Historic Places.

6-033. Frame wing, Broad Street Market, Harrisburg, Pennsylvania. Interior view. Allied Pix Service, 1974. P&P, HABS, PA, 22-HARBU, 4A-4.

6-034. Georgetown Market, Washington, D.C. Marc Blair, photographer, 1966. P&P,HABS,DC,GEO,82-1.

This market, built in 1865, is now occupied by Dean and DeLuca, a retail outlet specializing in fine foods and kitchenware.

6-035. Western Market, Washington, D.C. William Edmund Barrett, photographer, 1965. P&P,Goode G-2987X. LC-DIG-ppmsca-12496.

Western Market, once located at Twenty-First and K streets, NW, was designed by the City Architect in 1871. It was demolished in 1967.

6-036. Eastern Market, Washington, D.C. Jack E. Boucher, photographer, 1972. P&P,HABS,DC,WASH,415-1.

Eastern Market is one of three market houses designed by Adolf Cluss (see also 4-036, 7-020). Cluss worked on the project in his capacity as the city's engineer and member of the Board of Public Works in the early 1870s. Constructed in 1872–1873, Eastern Market still stands on Seventh Street between C Street and North Carolina Avenue, SE, in the heart of Capitol Hill. Lacking the architectural elaboration and scale required at Center Market, Eastern Market was noted for its economy of construction, unostentatious design, and standardized architectural vocabulary. The original brick building was approximately 180 feet long (20 bays) and 50 feet wide (5 bays) and covered an area of around 10,000 square feet (about one-sixth the size of Center Market). Cluss made generous use of the round arch style, which features prominently in the alternating windows and doorways. A detached open shed for farmers runs the length of the Seventh Street facade. The interior was heavily damaged by fire on April 30, 2007. A plan is under way to fully restore the building over the course of the next two years.

6-034

6-035

6-036

6-037

6-038

6-039

6-037. Detail, east side, central section, cornice, Eastern Market, Washington, D.C. Jack E. Boucher, photographer, 1972. P&P,HABS,DC,WASH,415-6.

Three projecting entrance bays are capped by massive brackets carrying a deep, overhanging cornice.

6-038. Interior, Eastern Market, Washington, D.C. Jack E. Boucher, photographer, 1972. P&P,HABS,DC,WASH,415-10.

Inside, Eastern Market features an open, three-story plan with iron-bar trusses supporting an exposed ceiling.

6-039. North Side Market, Pittsburgh, Pennsylvania. Unidentified photographer, ca. 1900–1910. P&P,DETR,LC-D4-36463.

This brick market was built around 1865, with mezzanine rooms added in 1934. It is approximately 202 feet square and consists of a one-story section surrounding a two-story central section with hip roof, dome, and cupola. Barrel vaults intersect at the corners and cover the one-story section. Primarily Italianate in style, the exterior details include a brick chevron pattern along the cornice and various arched and circular windows. Iron roof trusses are exposed on the interior.

6-040. Old Farmers' Market, Petersburg, Virginia. George Eisenman, photographer, 1968. P&P,HABS,VA,27-PET,26-2.

Major B. J. Black, architect, designed this octagonal market house in 1879. It was equipped with twenty butcher stalls that surrounded a large refrigerator in the center. The meat stalls were so arranged as to give all the butchers equal advantage. The shed also accommodated hucksters and fish dealers. The building still operates as a seasonal farmers' market.

6-041. Old Farmers' Market, Petersburg, Virginia. George Eisenman, photographer, 1968. P&P,HABS,VA,27-PET,26-3.

6-042. Detail of cast-iron brackets supporting the canopy roof, Old Farmers' Market, Petersburg, Virginia. George Eisenman, photographer, 1968. P&P,HABS,VA,27-PET,26-4.

6-040

6-041

6-042

6-043

6-045

6-044

6-043. City Market, Indianapolis, Indiana. Jack E. Boucher, photographer, 1970. P&P,HAER,IND,49-IND,14-9.

City Market was built in 1886 and designed by Diedrich A. Bohlen (1827–1890), a native of Hanover, Germany. After studying architecture at Holzminden, Bohlen traveled and worked in Europe before moving to the United States in 1852. Bohlen's City Market is an iron frame building with brick walls, limestone trim, and stone foundations. The floors were constructed of poured Portland cement, and Bohlen's drawings showed a layout of 196 stalls. The most distinctive feature is the interior space, created by twelve light-weight iron trusses—known as Fink trusses after Albert Fink (1827–1897), the German-born American railroad engineer—carried by fluted iron columns, fabricated by the Indianapolis firm of Hetherington and Berner. The Fink trusses, which span 60 feet, form a 200-foot-long nave, and the side-aisle trusses form an aisle space of 18 feet 6 inches. On March 27, 1974, the market house was listed on the National Register of Historic Landmarks. It was restored in 1977 and is still in operation.

6-044. City Market, Indianapolis, Indiana. Jack E. Boucher, photographer, 1970. P&P,HABS,IND,49-IND,14-3.

6-045. Interior toward the south, City Market, Indianapolis, Indiana. Jack E. Boucher, photographer, 1970. P&P,HABS,IND,49-IND,14-5.

6-046

6-047

6-046. Detail view showing column capitals and support bracing for roof truss structure, City Market, Indianapolis, Indiana. Jack E. Boucher, photographer, 1974. P&P,HAER,IND,49-IND,6-12.

6-047. Fruit vendors in City Market, Indianapolis, Indiana. Lewis Wickes Hine, photographer, 1908. P&P,NCLC,LC-DIG-nclc-03212.

6-048

6-049

6-050

6-048. City Market, Kansas City, Missouri. Benjamin Kilburn, stereographer, 1890. P&P,LC-USZ6-141.

6-049. Central Market, Lancaster, Pennsylvania. Marjory Collins, photographer, 1942. P&P,FSA/OWI,LC-USW3-010975-E.

6-050. Central Market, Lancaster, Pennsylvania. Marjory Collins, photographer, 1942. P&P,FSA/OWI,LC-USW3-010974-E.

Central Market was designed by James H. Warner and erected in 1889. The structure measures 140 by 175 feet and was originally designed for 252 stalls constructed of yellow pine. The pressed brick facade features two towers, 72 feet high, flanking a central gable that displays a checkerboard pattern at the peak. Interior light is furnished by ranges of small hipped dormers. The Lancaster Central Market is in excellent condition and still operates as a public market.

6-051

6-051. City Market, Kansas City, Missouri. Unidentified photographer, 1906. P&P,DETR,LC-D401-19219.

6-052. Edw. Neumann, Broadway Market, Detroit, Michigan. Unidentified photographer, ca. 1905–1915. P&P,DETR,LC-D4-43793.

Neumann upgraded his fruit stand with the installation of refrigerated glass cases.

6-053. Edw. Neumann, Broadway Market, Detroit, Michigan. Unidentified photographer, ca. 1905–1915. P&P,DETR,LC-D4-43794.

6-052

6-053

MARKET HOUSE COMPANIES

Discontented with the "old-fashioned" public markets, businessmen and real estate developers in the mid-nineteenth century promoted market houses that were owned and managed by private companies. With their legal authority to issue stock, market house companies raised the much-needed capital for property and new buildings, including the latest technological innovations in refrigeration, lighting, and construction. Officers and stockholders were typically merchants who participated financially in the affairs of the market. For example, in 1873 a group of butchers from Center Market in Washington, D.C., formed their own company and built the Northern Liberty Market, designed by James H. McGill, a local architect and builder (6-055–6-058). Similarly, in Philadelphia, there were at least five substantial market houses under the management of private corporations, including the Farmers' Market (6-054) and the Ridge Avenue Farmers' Market (6-059–6-060).

6-054. Farmers' Market, Philadelphia, Pennsylvania. Samuel Sloan (1815–1884), architect, 1860. From Earl Shinn, *A Century After: Picturesque Glimpses of Philadelphia and Pennsylvania* (1875), p. 156. Gen. Coll.,F185.5.S2. LC-DIG-ppmsca-12673.

INTERIOR FARMERS' MARKET.

the market-house on High street, adjoining the Court-house, where the sight of stocks, posts, and pillory reminded evil-doers of the punishments that awaited them.

6-054

6-055. Northern Liberty Market, Washington, D.C. Unidentified photographer, 1928. P&P,Goode,LOT 11800-J2,G-1625. LC-DIG-ppmsca-12495.

In 1874 a private company of dealers hired James H. McGill to construct this market on the block bound by Fourth and Fifth and K and L streets, NW. Also known as Convention Hall Market or Savage Square Market, it stood 85 feet high and measured 126 feet wide by 324 feet long. It was destroyed by fire in 1946.

6-056. Interior of the Northern Liberty Market, Washington, D.C. James H. McGill, architect, ca. 1875. Courtesy of the Columbia Historical Society. P&P,Goode,LOT 11800-J2,G-695. LC-DIG-ppmsca-12494.

The roof was supported by fourteen arched iron trusses, each a single span of 126 feet. The floor was paved with North River bluestone. Five wide aisles extended the length of the building, and fifteen aisles ran the width. The market was equipped with 284 stalls.

6-055

6-056

6-057. Northern Liberty Market, Washington, D.C., during the fire. Unidentified photographer, March 1, 1946. P&P,Goode G-717,LC-G7-717. LC-DIG-ppm-sca-12489.

6-058. Remains after the fire, Northern Liberty Market, Washington, D.C. Unidentified photographer, March 1, 1946. P&P,Goode G-716,LC-G7-716. LC-DIG-ppm-sca-12488.

6-059. Ridge Avenue Farmers' Market, Philadelphia, Pennsylvania. David E. Supplee, architect. Jack E. Boucher, photographer, 1973. P&P,HABS,PA,51-PHILA,558-3.

A private company built this brick market house in 1875. It measured 93 by 260 feet and was noted for its timber roof framing that combined the king post truss with the hammer beam trusses that supported a catwalk. The interior was lighted by four long shed dormers on each side of the steeply pitched, jerkin head (clipped gable) roof. The original roofing material was slate. In March 1997, after years of neglect, the roof collapsed from a storm and the building was demolished.

6-060. Ridge Avenue Farmers' Market, Philadelphia, Pennsylvania. Jack E. Boucher, photographer, 1973. P&P,HABS,PA,51-PHILA,558-4.

6-061. Philadelphia and Reading Railroad, Terminal Station, Philadelphia, Pennsylvannia. Unidentified photographer, 1893. P&P,HABS,PA,51-PHILA,521-1.

Reading Terminal Market was constructed in 1891–1892 underneath the train shed of the new railroad terminal. The original interior was divided into approximately seven hundred iron stalls, and beneath the cement floor was an extensive basement with cork-insulated cold storage. The huge complex had its own generating and steam heating facilities. The Reading Terminal Market was incorporated into the Pennsylvania Convention Center in the early 1990s and continues to attract shoppers and tourists today.

6-059

6-060

6-061

6·062

6·063

6-062. Philadelphia and Reading Railroad, Terminal Station, Philadelphia, Pennsylvania. Detail of northeast corner with market sign. Jack E. Boucher, photographer, 1974. P&P,HABS,PA,51-PHILA,521-4.

6-063. Margerum's Old Fashion Corner, Reading Terminal Market, Philadelphia, Pennsylvania. Jet Lowe, photographer, 1991. P&P,HAER,PA,51-PHILA,711-16.

6-064

6-064. City Market, Ninth and San Pedro streets, Los Angeles, California. Morgan, Walls & Clements, architects. T. Utsushigawa, photographer, 1910. P&P,LC-USZ62-50999 and 51000.

A corporation called the City Market of Los Angeles constructed this mission-style market in 1909. It was noted for its solid reinforced concrete construction.

6-065. Pike Place Market, Seattle, Washington. From Arthur Goodwin, *Markets: Public and Private*, (1929), p. 73. Gen. Coll.,HF5470.G6. LC-DIG-ppmsca-12862.

Arthur Goodwin (1887–ca. 1960) provided most of the design work for the market complex from 1907 to the mid-1920s. Four distinct markets made up the complex: the Economy Public Market, the Outlook Public Market, the Pike Place Public Market, and the Municipal Market. Of these facilities, only the North Arcade addition to the Pike Place Public Market had been built with public funds. Pike Place Market is now a seven-acre historic district and is one of the leading tourist attractions in Seattle. Photograph courtesy Seattle Municipal Archives, item no. 33283.

6-066. Manning's Market (now Lowell's Cafe), Pike Place Market, Seattle, Washington, 1924. From Arthur Goodwin, *Markets: Public and Private* (1929), p. 172. Gen. Coll.,HF5470.G6. LC-DIG-ppmsca-12869. Photograph courtesy Seattle Municipal Archives, item no. 35885.

6-065

6-066

MUNICIPAL MARKETS IN THE TWENTIETH CENTURY

Two distinct phases of new market construction emerged in the United States during the twentieth century. The first phase began in the 1890s and continued into the 1920s, when progressives and municipal reformers looked for ways to improve the quality of urban life through improved public markets. They also believed that modern, attractive markets, among other things, would contribute to improving the city's national and international image. This belief was part of the larger City Beautiful movement, whose promoters hoped that physical improvements would inculcate citizens with moral values and civic pride. A new style dictated by new materials, such as concrete, steel, tile, marble, and glass, along with brick, would meet the demand for aesthetic appeal, durability, and sanitation.

The second phase occurred during the Great Depression, when communities—both rural and urban—discovered that public markets were more efficient than chain grocery stores in promoting direct marketing between consumer and producer. Driven by a desire to eliminate the cost of the middleman, cities as far ranging as New York City and Du Bois, Pennsylvania, to Nashville, Tennessee, and Austin, Texas, took advantage of New Deal support to build new market houses. Local taste and circumstances dictated a variety of styles and materials for market houses that ranged from the brick colonial revival City Market in Nashville, Tennessee (6-087), to the streamlined, reinforced concrete neighborhood markets built in New York City (6-090–6-091).

opposite

6-067. General view and first floor plans, Market house for City of Pittsburgh, Pennsylvania. Alden & Harlow, architects. From *American Architect* 95 (March 10, 1909): pt. 1, n. 1733, pl.fol. p. 88. MMRC, Microfilm 05422, no. 628.

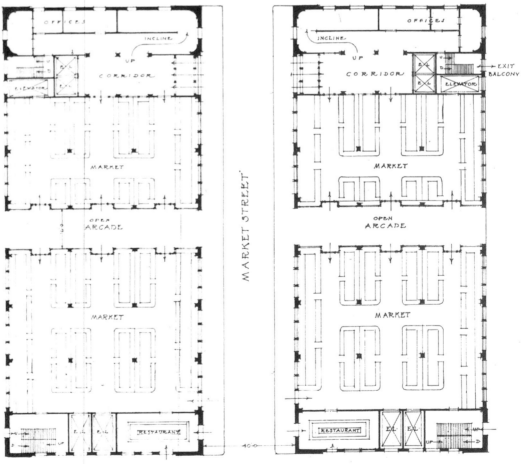

·FIRST·FLOOR·

MARKET HOUSE FOR
CITY OF PITTSBURG, PA

MESSRS. ALDEN & HARLOW
ARCHITECTS

6-067

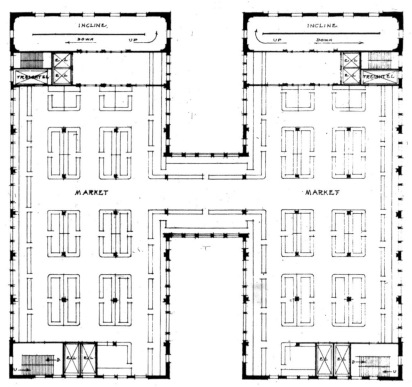

·THIRD·FLOOR·

·SECOND·FLOOR·

MARKET HOUSE FOR
CITY OF PITTSBURG, PA.

MESSRS. ALDEN & HARLOW
ARCHITECTS

6-068. Second and third floor plans, Market house for City of Pittsburgh, Pennsylvania. Alden & Harlow, architects. From *American Architect* 95 (March 10, 1909): pt. 1, n. 1733, pl.fol. p. 88. MMRC, Microfilm 05422, no. 628.

6-068

6-069

6-070

6-071

6-069. City Market, Brownsville, Texas. Arthur Rothstein, photographer, 1942. P&P,FSA/OWI,LC-USF34-022084-D.

6-070. City Market, Brownsville, Texas. Arthur Rothstein, photographer, 1942. P&P,FSA/OWI,LC-USF34-022083-D.

6-071. City Market, Brownsville, Texas. Arthur Rothstein, photographer, 1942. P&P,FSA/OWI,LC-USF34-022058-D.

6-072. City Market, San Antonio, Texas. Unidentified photographer, 1905. P&P,Postcards,PR06(AA)CN 038,Box 3. LC-DIG-ppm-sca-12807.

City Market was designed by Alfred Giles (1853–1920), architect, in 1899. Considered a modern municipal market in its day, the building was equipped with refrigeration, running water, and a second-floor auditorium for public concerts, boxing matches, and political rallies. After a period of decline, the market was demolished in 1938 and replaced by the Farmer's Market (6-095).

6-072

6-073

6-074

6-075

6-073. Municipal Public Market, Birmingham, Alabama. From Arthur Goodwin, *Markets: Public and Private* (1929), p. 155. Gen. Coll.,HF5470.G6. LC-DIG-ppmsca-12867.

6-074. Interior view, Municipal Public Market, Birmingham, Alabama. From Arthur Goodwin, *Markets: Public and Private* (1929), p. 152. Gen. Coll.,HF5470.G6. LC-DIG-ppmsca-12866.

6-075. General view, Municipal Market, Evansville, Indiana. Clifford Shopbell & Company, architects. From *Western Architect* 28 (March 1919): detail, plate 15. Gen. Coll.,NA1.W4. LC-DIG-ppmsca-12681.

6-076. Interior, Municipal Market, Evansville, Indiana. From *Western Architect* 28 (March 1919): detail, plate 15. Gen. Coll.,NA1.W4. LC-DIG-ppmsca-12682.

6-077. One of the Diamond Square market houses, Pittsburgh, Pennsylvania. Rutan & Russell, architects. From *Architecture and Building* 48 (June 1916): plate 32. Gen. Coll.,NA1.A48. LC-DIG-ppmsca-12685.

6-078. Municipal Fish Market, Washington, D.C. Unidentified photographer, ca. 1920. P&P,Geog File-Washington,D.C.-Commerce-Food-Stores. LC-DIG-ppmsca-12315.

The Municipal Fish Market was built in the Colonial Revival style in 1916, according to the plans of the city architect, Snowden Ashford. The rear of the market faced the Washington waterfront and housed several seafood restaurants. The building was razed in 1960 due to urban renewal.

6-076

6-077

6-078

6-079

6-080

6-080

6-079. Wooden structure housing the Tri-County Farmers Co-operative Market at Du Bois, Pennsylvania. The farmers hope in time to be able to erect a brick building. Jack Delano, photographer, 1940. P&P,FSA/OWI,LC-USF34-041320-D.

6-080. Public Market, Portland, Oregon. Arthur Rothstein, photographer, 1936. P&P,FSA/OWI,LC-USF34- 005146-E.

In 1929 the city of Portland began negotiating with the Public Market Company of Portland to construct a massive marketplace on the waterfront, in an effort to replace the municipally owned Carroll Market. Delayed by the Depression, construction did not begin until 1933, with assistance from the Reconstruction Finance Corporation. The architects were Lawrence, Holford and Allyn; structural engineer, Howard Rigler; supervising architect, Sydney B. Hayslip; market consultant, Arthur Goodwin; and general contractor, Ross B. Hammond, Inc.

Thirty-one islands and a perimeter of shops provided counter space for 120 vendors on the ground floor, along with 298 stalls for farmers renting on a daily basis. The mezzanine contained shops, restaurants, and an auditorium; the second floor was for parking and cold storage. The main roof was used for open-air parking and for enclosed dry storage. Because the market was unable to sustain enough patronage, the building was leased for other purposes in the 1940s. In 1969 it was demolished to make way for the McCall Waterfront Park.

6-081. Interior of Tri-County Farmers Co-operative Market at Du Bois, Pennsylvania. Jack Delano, photographer, 1940. P&P,FSA/OWI,LC-USF34-041286-D.

6-082. Customers at the entrance of the Tri-County Farmers Co-operative Market in Du Bois, Pennsylvania. Jack Delano, photographer, 1940. P&P,FSA/OWI,LC-USF34-041392-E.

6-083. The Farmers Market, San Antonio, Texas. Russell Lee, photographer, 1939. P&P,FSA/OWI,LC-USF34-032645-D.

The structure was built in 1938. It was renovated in the 1970s by the San Antonio Development Agency and converted into El Mercado, a bazaar with specialty shops.

6-084. Unloading trucks at vegetable market. San Antonio, Texas. Russell Lee, photographer, 1939. P&P,FSA/OWI,LC-USF34-032687-D.

6-083

6-082

6-084

6-085

6-086

6-087

6-085. Interior, City Market, Nashville, Tennessee. Public Works Administration, 1937. P&P,NA712.A5 1939(Case Y). LC-DIG-ppmsca-12658.

6-086. City Market, Austin, Texas. Public Works Administration, 1935. P&P,NA712.A5 1939(Case Y). LC-DIG-ppmsca-12657.

The market was built of reinforced concrete, with some brick and glass. Four covered sheds radiated from a central pavilion, in which offices and a restaurant were located.

6-087. General view, City Market, Nashville, Tennessee. Public Works Administration, 1937. P&P,NA712.A5 1939(Case Y). LC-DIG-ppmsca-12659.

opposite
6-088. Interior, City Market, Austin, Texas. Public Works Administration, 1935. P&P,NA712.A5 1939(Case Y). LC-DIG-ppmsca-12648.

6-088

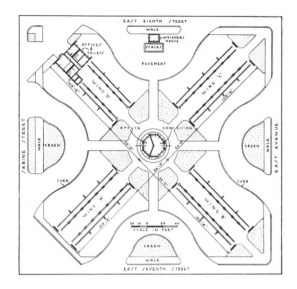

6-089

6-089. Site plan, City Market, Austin, Texas. Public Works Administration, 1935. From C. W. Short and R. Stanley-Brown, *Public Buildings: A Survey of Architecture of Projects Constructed by Federal and Other Governmental Bodies between the Years 1933 and 1939* (Washington, DC: Public Works Administration, 1939), p. 631. Gen. Coll.,NA4208.A4. LC-DIG-ppmsca-12656.

6-090. Thirteenth Avenue Retail Market, between 39th and 42nd streets, Brooklyn, New York, New York. Walter Albertin, photographer. P&P,NYWTS,Subj/Geog File-Markets-Thirteenth Avenue Market. LC-DIG-ppmsca-12723.

This was one of a series of small neighborhood retail markets designed and built by the Department of Markets of the City of New York. The one-story brick building was 15,000 square feet in area and contained 137 stands when it opened in October 1939. Construction was funded in part by a grant from the Public Works Administration. The building is now used as a grocery store.

6-091. First Avenue Retail Market, New York, New York. Jack O'Brien, photographer, 1967. P&P,NYWTS,Subj/Geog File-Markets-First Avenue Market. LC-DIG-ppmsca-12752.

The market, located at Tenth Street, was designed and built by the Department of Markets of the City of New York in 1938. It was intended to replace the First Avenue pushcart market that extended from First to Fourteenth streets. The building is now used as a neighborhood theater.

6-090

6-091

6-092

6-093

6-094

6-095

6-092. Italian meat stall in the First Avenue Market, New York, New York. Marjory Collins, photographer, 1943. P&P,FSA/OWI,LC-USW3-014483-D.

6-093. Fish merchant in the First Avenue Market, New York, New York. Marjory Collins, photographer, 1943. P&P,FSA/OWI,LC-USW3-014501-D.

6-094. Italian grocer in the First Avenue Market, New York, New York. Marjory Collins, photographer, 1943. P&P,FSA/OWI,LC-USW3-014502-D.

6-095. Italian and Jewish customers in the First Avenue Market, New York, New York. Marjory Collins, photographer, 1943. P&P,FSA/OWI,LC-USW3-014470-D.

6-096. First Avenue Market, New York, New York. P&P,NYWTS,Subj/Geog-Markets-General. LC-DIG-ppmsca-12693. William F. Warnecke, photographer.

6-097. Public Market, First Avenue and 73rd Street, New York, New York. Gottscho-Schleisner, Inc., 1948. P&P,GSC,LC-G612-T-52627.

6-096

6-097

CENTRAL MARKETS

Central markets were conceived in the mid-nineteenth century, when railroads made it possible to transport large quantities of perishable food directly into the city centers. By bringing everything to one point, city officials believed that a central market could better regulate prices in the other markets and handle both wholesale and retail on such a scale as to ensure producers and dealers a large turnover of volume. The consumer would also benefit from the opportunity to find variety and quality at a reasonable price in one location—the same principles that encouraged development of the department store.

A central market was primarily a large retail and wholesale market that covered several city blocks under one roof or a series of roofs. It was centrally located near the greatest concentration of consumers and businesses and was accessible by major transportation routes. Considered a phenomenon of large cities with several market halls or markets, the central market was designed as the chief place of business in which, or from which, the wholesale food trade would develop. The concentration of sales on a large scale enabled the central market to serve both as a retail hall for the neighborhood in which it was erected and as a feeder market for subsidiary markets, grocery stores, restaurants, steamships, and other institutions that purchased in bulk.

Architects and engineers paid particular attention to traffic circulation, ample parking, the safeguarding of pedestrians, and access to major transportation routes including rail and water. Buildings equipped with stalls numbering in the hundreds required large covered spaces unencumbered by supports. Floor plans and furnishings were customized according to the type of trade. The concentration of so many vendors under one roof also demanded adjunct facilities, such as cold storage, refrigeration, ice plants, power plants, incinerators, and garbage disposals, as well as restaurants and restrooms.

Construction of central markets waned by the early twentieth century, when cities returned to a preference for decentralizing food marketing and distribution. A decline of subsidiary public markets and the growth of chain grocery stores and, later, supermarkets forced most cities to declare their central market obsolete. Typically the land was appropriated for other purposes and the wholesale trade in fresh food was transferred to new terminal markets located outside of the central business district. This chapter highlights three central markets that share nineteenth-century origins and similar fates: Les Halles Centrales in Paris, Center Market in Washington, D.C., and Washington Market in New York City.

7-001

7-001. Bird's-eye view, Les Halles, Paris, France. From V. Baltard and F. Callet, *Monographie des halles centrales de Paris* (1863), plate 1. P&P,LC-DC777.B19(Case Z). LC-DIG-ppmsca-12833.

The architects conceived of the market as a series of six-meter modules. The large pavilions were each nine modules square, and the small ones were seven modules square.

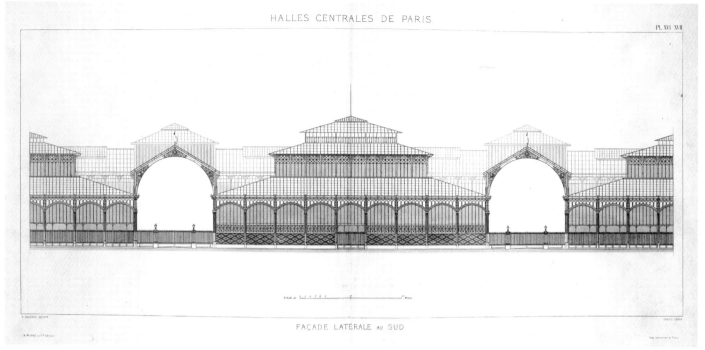

FAÇADE LATÉRALE AU SUD

7-002

7-002. Elevation, Les Halles, Paris, France. From V. Baltard and F. Callet, *Monographie des halles centrales de Paris* (1863), plate 16–17. P&P,LC-DC777.B19(Case Z). LC-DIG-ppmsca-12632.

All exterior supports were cast-iron columns engaged in pilasters, with two such engaged columns in every corner pilaster. Between these outer columns, which were hollow to carry off rainwater, a plinth of freestone supported a brick wall, which was topped with another course of stone supporting wooden frames with adjustable glass windows.

LES HALLES CENTRALES, PARIS

Les Halles, the central market for the city of Paris, was constructed in 1852–1859 according to the designs of Victor Baltard (1805–1874) and Felix-Emmanuel Callet (1791–1854). By 1870 Les Halles encompassed 20 acres, nearly half of which were covered by ten iron and glass pavilions terminating at the round grain market, the Halle au Blé. Beneath the entire complex were two underground levels—one for cellars and cold storage, and below that, another level for direct connection to the principal railway stations, a feature that was never utilized.

Les Halles had an immediate impact on the construction of new markets in Europe. The design was repeated over the next four to five decades all over Paris and in many other cities throughout France. The Parisian market type also was repeated outside of France, with similar versions for export. The great French iron foundry at Le Creusot, for example, exported prefabricated iron structures to many parts of the world, including the covered market in the Plaza de la Cebada in Madrid (see 6-002). Les Halles was demolished in the 1960s, except for one pavilion that was relocated to Nogent-sur-Marne, and the land was appropriated for retail development. All marketing activity moved to Rungis—today, the largest wholesale market in Europe.

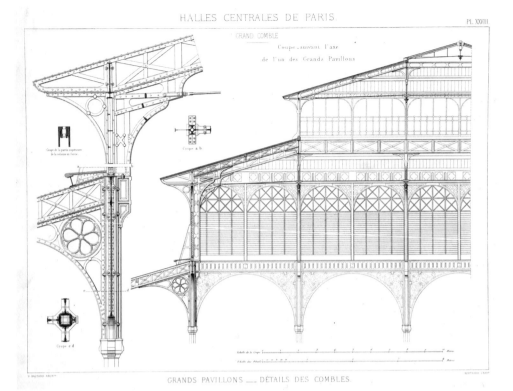

GRAND COMBLE

Coupe suivant l'axe

de l'un des Grands Pavillons

GRANDS PAVILLONS — DÉTAILS DES COMBLES.

7-003

7-003. Truss details, Les Halles, Paris, France. From V. Baltard and F. Callet, *Monographie des halles centrales de Paris* (1863), plate 28. P&P,LC-DC777.B19(Case Z). LC-DIG-ppmsca-12633.

Exterior columns joined with trellis wall plates supported the trellis rafters of the shed roofs.

7-004. Floor plan, eastern part, Les Halles, Paris, France. From V. Baltard and F. Callet, *Monographie des halles centrales de Paris* (1863), plate 11, detail. P&P,LC-DC777.B19(Case Z). LC-DIG-ppmsca-12631.

Each pavilion was dedicated to the sale of certain goods. Clockwise from upper left are Pavilion 7 (fruit and flowers); Pavilion 9 (fish); Pavilion 11 (wild game and oysters); Pavilion 8 (vegetables); Pavilion 10 (wholesale butter, eggs, and cheese); and Pavilion 12 (retail foods).

opposite
7-005. Public scales, meat pavilion, Les Halles, Paris, France. From V. Baltard and F. Callet, *Monographie des halles centrales de Paris* (1863), plate 33. detail. P&P,LC-DC777.B19(Case Z). LC-DIG-ppmsca-12635.

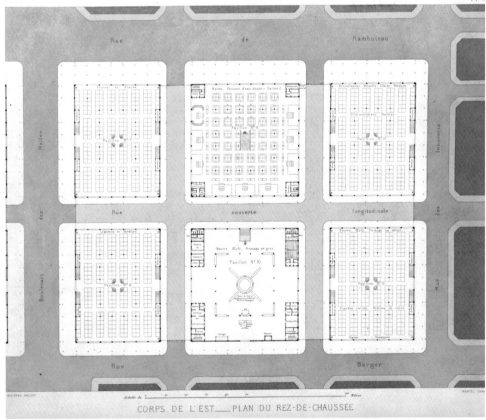

CORPS DE L'EST — PLAN DU REZ-DE-CHAUSSÉE.

7-004

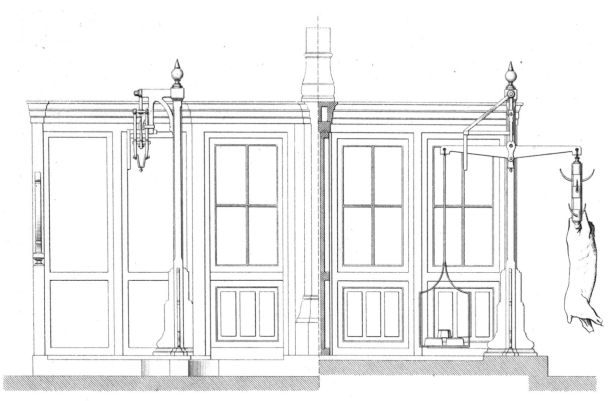

Façade par moitié.   Coupe sur AB.

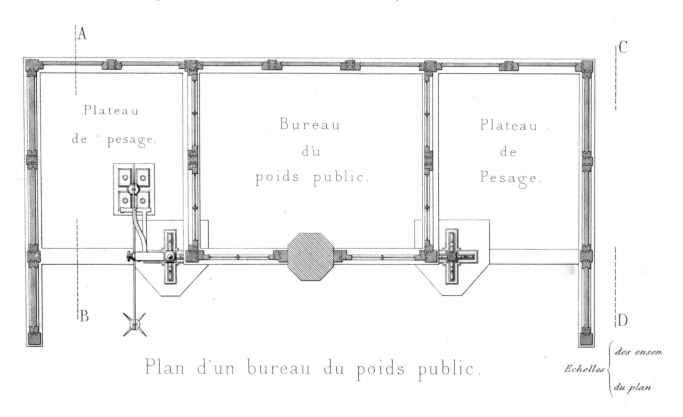

Plan d'un bureau du poids public.

Plateau
de pesage.

Bureau
du
poids public.

Plateau
de
Pesage.

Echelles { des ensem.

{ du plan

7-005

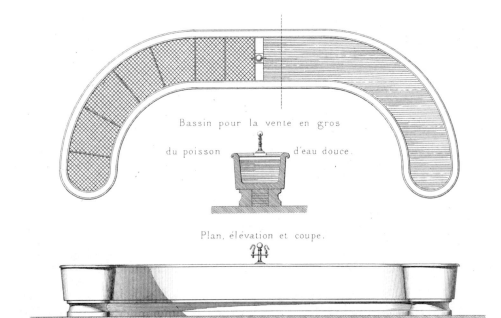

Bassin pour la vente en gros

du poisson   d'eau douce.

Plan, élévation et coupe.

7-006

HALLES CENTRALES DE PARIS.   PL. XXXV

DÉTAILS DES APPAREILS POUR L'EAU ET POUR LE GAZ.

7-007

7-006. Basin for the sale of live fish, Les Halles, Paris, France. From V. Baltard and F. Callet, *Monographie des halles centrales de Paris* (1863), plate 31. P&P,LC-DC777.B19(Case Z). LC-DIG-ppmsca-12634.

7-007. Details of water and gas fixtures, Les Halles, Paris, France. From V. Baltard and F. Callet, *Monographie des halles centrales de Paris* (1863), plate 35. P&P,LC-DC777.B19(Case Z). LC-DIG-ppmsca-12637.

7-008

7-009

7-008. Market porter, Les Halles, Paris, France. Brassaï, photographer, 1939. P&P,LC-USZ62-121103.

Brassaï was the pseudonym of Gyula Halász (1899–1984).

7-009. Porter, Les Halles, Paris, France. Unidentified photographer, 1946. Corbis. P&P,NYWTS,Subj/Geog-France-Paris-Markets. LC-DIG-ppmsca-12686.

Porters, also known as huskies, in the fish section of Les Halles wore special hats, different from the wide-brimmed headgear worn in the other sections of the market (7-012). This fish porter balances a crate atop his narrow-brimmed, hard-crowned hat.

7-010. Woman weighing produce with a hand-held scale at the Halles Centrales, Paris, France. Marcus J. Clark, photographer, 1939. P&P,LC-USZ62-95982.

7-010

7-011

7-012

7-011. Buyers in the game section of Les Halles, Paris, France. From Mrs. Elmer Black, *A Terminal Market System: New York's Most Urgent Need* (1912), p. 26. Gen. Coll.,HF5470.B5. LC-DIG-ppmsca-12679.

The official porters of the market are identified by their wide-brimmed hats.

7-012. Les Halles, Paris, France. Marcus J. Clark, photographer, 1939. P&P,LC-USZ62-95981.

CENTER MARKET, WASHINGTON, D.C.

After the Civil War, the U.S. federal government was determined to have a modern market house on Pennsylvania Avenue—one that would place Washington, D.C., among the ranks of the great European capitals. A new Center Market became a reality when Congress authorized an act to incorporate the Washington Market Company on May 20, 1870. The company was empowered to construct and manage a new market in place of the old municipal market (7-014) that stood on the original market squares.

Adolf Cluss (1825–1905), architect for the Washington Market Company, conceived of the project as a series of four buildings arranged in a square around an open court. The market was built in stages from 1872 to 1878, beginning with three market wings on Seventh, Ninth, and B (now Constitution Avenue) streets, and ending with a row of wholesale stores facing Pennsylvania Avenue. In addition to solid construction and fireproofing, Cluss carefully considered the classification of space by goods, separate facilities for the wholesale and retail trade, parking for farmers' wagons, the availability of meeting space, restrooms, offices, ventilation, state-of-the-art refrigeration, and cold storage facilities.

Center Market was a victim of plans to build a core of monumental government buildings on Pennsylvania Avenue between the Capitol and the White House. It was demolished in 1931 to provide a site for the National Archives.

7-013. Plan of Center Market Square, Washington, D.C. Frederick C. De Krafft (?), draftsman, ca. 1826. G&M,G3852.C4 182-.P5 Vault,detail.

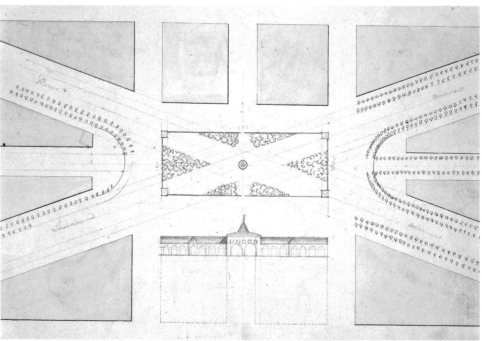

7-013

7-014

7-015

7-014. Center Market, Washington, D.C.
Joseph E. Bishop, photographer, 1865.
P&P,LC-DIG-ppmsc-09958.

The first substantial building on the site was
this low, whitewashed shed.

7-015. Center Market, Washington, D.C.
Unidentified photographer, ca. 1910–1930.
P&P,LC-USZ62-114760.

7-016

7-016. Row of stores, including Armour Company, north facade, Center Market, Washington, D.C. Commercial Photo Company, ca. 1910. P&P,Goode G-1696,LC-G7-1696. LC-DIG-ppmsca-12478.

7-017. Plaque on the front of Center Market, Washington, D.C. P&P,Goode G-1714,LC-G7-1714. LC-DIG-ppmsca-12481.

7-018. Center Market, Washington, D.C. Unidentified photographer, ca. 1915. From Columbia Historical Society. P&P,Goode G-3945X,LC-USZ62-102699.

7-019. Row of stores, north facade, Center Market, Washington, D.C. Commercial Photo Company, ca. 1910. P&P,Goode G-1861,LC-G7-1861. LC-DIG-ppmsca-12483.

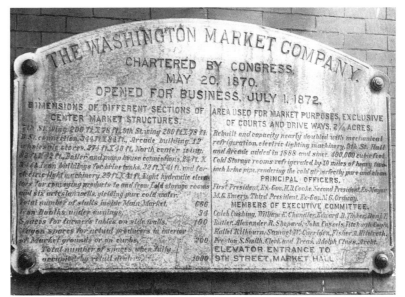

7-017

7-018

7-019

7-020

7-020. North facade, flanking Seventh Street, Center Market, Washington, D.C. Unidentified photographer, ca. 1900. P&P, Goode G-4492X, LC-USZ62-113937.

7-021. North facade, flanking Ninth Street, Center Market, Washington, D.C. Commercial Photo Company, 1920. P&P, Goode G-1695, LC-G7-1695. LC-DIG-ppmsca-12477.

7-021

7-022. Armour & Company, Center Market, Washington, D.C. Unidentified photographer, ca. 1885. P&P,LC-USZ62-26704.

The Washington Market Company lured two important tenants to the wholesale section of Center Market—Armour and Swift. Both companies were among the nation's largest wholesale dealers in Chicago dressed beef.

7-023. West (Ninth Street) facade, Center Market, Washington, D.C. Unidentified photographer, ca. 1910. P&P,Goode G-1712,LC-G7-1712. LC-DIG-ppmsca-12480.

7-024. Ground floor plan, Center Market, Washington, D.C. From U.S. Senate Committee on the District of Columbia, *Papers Relating to the Washington Market Company, 60th Cong. 1st sess. S.Doc. 495*, 1908. Gen. Coll.,HF5472.U7W36. LC-DIG-ppmsca-12644.

Center Market contained 666 retail stalls, which varied in size and character according to the needs of the different trades. Butcher stalls were 48 square feet, compared to 36 square feet for butter stalls; the most moderate stalls were for bacon dealers and hucksters.

7-022

7-023

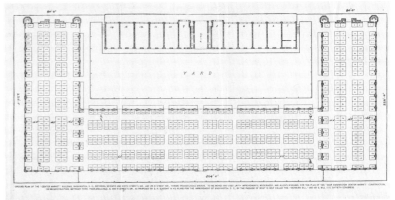

7-024

7-025

7-026

7-027

7-025. Center Market, Washington, D.C. Unidentified photographer, ca. 1909—1932. P&P,LC-USZ62-94730.

7-026. Baker's stall, Center Market, Washington, D.C. Unidentified photographer, ca. 1915. P&P,Goode G-1697,LC-G7-1697. LC-DIG-ppmsca-12479.

The "tasty modern market stalls," as they were described in the company charter, had uniform overhead signs that identified the stall number and vendor.

7-027. South facade, Center Market, Washington, D.C. Unidentified photographer, ca. 1875. P&P,Goode G-3514X,LC-G7-3514X.

7-028

7-028. Vendor, Center Market, Washington, D.C. Unidentified photographer, ca. 1890. P&P,Goode G-877,LC-G7-877. LC-DIG-ppmsca-12491.

Outside of the market, the country people, as they were often called, furnished their own benches under the eaves and awnings, where they occupied their spaces for a nominal daily fee.

7-029. Center Market, Washington, D.C. Unidentified photographer, ca. 1900. From Columbia Historical Society. P&P,Goode G-600X. LC-DIG-ppmsca-09959.

7-030. Center Market, Washington, D.C. Theodor Horydczak, photographer, ca. 1920–1931. P&P,LC-H814-T-1029.

7-029

7-030

7-031

7-031. Center Market, Washington, D.C. Theodor Horydczak, photographer, ca. 1920–1931. P&P,LC-H814-T-1030.

7-032. Constitution Avenue facade, Center Market, Washington, D.C. Leet Brothers, ca. 1929. P&P,Goode G-2341,LC-G7-2341. LC-DIG-ppmsca-12484.

7-033. Men's comfort station, Center Market, Washington, D.C. Unidentified photographer, ca. 1910–1930. From Smithsonian Institution. P&P,Goode G-3516X,LC-USZ62-97022.

7-032

7-033

7-034. Sheds at Tenth Street, NW., Center Market, Washington, D.C. Unidentified photographer, ca. 1929. P&P,Goode G-886,LC-G7-886. LC-DIG-ppmsca-12492.

7-035. View looking northeast, Center Market, Washington, D.C. Unidentified photographer, ca. 1925–1930. P&P,Goode G-811,LC-G7-811. LC-DIG-ppmsca-12490.

7-036. Sheds at Tenth Street, NW, Center Market, Washington, D.C. Unidentified photographer, 1915. P&P,Goode G-2701X,LC-G7-2701. LC-DIG-ppmsca-12485.

7-034

7-035

7-036

7-037

7-037. Wholesale sheds, Center Market, Washington, D.C. Clifton Adams, photographer, 1923. From National Geographic Society. P&P,Goode G-927X. LC-DIG-ppm-sca-12493.

7-038. Razing of wing near Tenth Street, NW, Center Market, Washington, D.C. Unidentified photographer, ca. 1930. P&P,Goode G-1740,LC-G7-1740. LC-DIG-ppmsca-12482.

Wholesale row between Tenth and Twelfth streets was demolished in 1930 to make way for the development of Federal Triangle.

7-038

Washington Market, established in 1812, was located on the west side of lower Manhattan, on the block bound by Washington, West, Fulton, and Vesey streets. By 1858 it was the largest market in the United States, including not only the retail market building but also the row of wholesale stores that developed northward along the Hudson River (7-050–7-054). It also included West Washington Market, which was established on adjacent landfill in order to accommodate farmers bringing country produce (7-047–7-048). The retail building was replaced in 1884, renovated in 1913, and remodeled in 1940.

As with other central markets, Washington Market was a victim of urban renewal. The retail building was closed in 1956, auctioned off for private development in 1958, and demolished in 1960. The dislocation of merchants, along with the associated wholesale trade in the neighborhood, forced the city to plan a replacement market at Hunt's Point (see 8-047–8-053). The block on which Washington Market stood eventually was incorporated into the World Trade Center.

7-039. *Washington Market, New York, New York*. From *Gleason's Pictorial Drawing-Room Companion*, March 5, 1853. P&P,AP2.B227(Case Y). LC-DIG-ppmsca-12638.

The first substantial market on the site was built in 1812 in the popular neoclassical style. By 1853 there were more than 500 stalls in Washington Market and an additional 400 stalls in West Washington Market, located on adjacent landfill.

REPRESENTATION OF THE FAMOUS WASHINGTON MARKET, NEW YORK CITY.

7-039

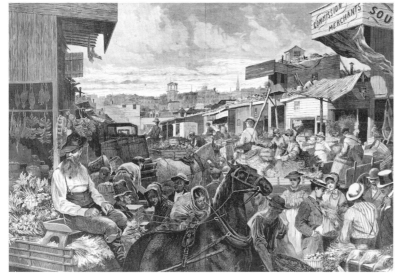

7-040

7-041

7-042

7-043

7-040. *Washington Market, New York, 1872.* Wood engraving after Tavernier. From *Harper's Weekly* 16 (November 30, 1872), Supplement: 940–41. P&P,LC-USZ62-83494.

By the 1870s, newspapers and popular journals criticized the chaos and disorder at New York's public markets, especially Washington Market—the city's largest.

7-041. Washington Market, New York, New York. Unidentified photographer, 1912. P&P,NYWTS,Subj/Geog-Markets-Washington Market-Retail. LC-DIG-ppmsca-12744.

The old Washington Market was replaced with a new market designed by Douglas Smyth and opened in 1884. This view was taken during the renovations of 1912–1913. Photo caption reads: "Washington Market Centennial. 1812–1912. Showing outside sheds removed by President McAneny, also new window fronts affording light and air for interiors, and the sidewalk restored to the public."

7-042. *Washington Market, New York.* W. P. Snyder, engraver, 1882. P&P,NYWTS,Subj/Geog-Markets-Washington Market-Retail. LC-DIG-ppmsca-12739.

7-043. Butchers celebrating the opening of Washington Market, New York, New York. From *Frank Leslie's,* December 27, 1884. MMRC,Microfilm 02282.

7-044. Housewives' League at Washington Market, New York, New York. Bain News Service, N.Y.C., ca. 1910. P&P,LC-USZ62-70775.

7-045. Washington Market, New York, New York. Unidentified photographer, 1915. P&P,NYWTS,Subj/Geog-Markets-Washington Market-Retail. LC-DIG-ppmsca-12743.

The 1884 market house was renovated in 1913, when it received its first coat of paint since construction. At the same time, it received a major interior overhaul that included a new concrete floor, terrazzo aisles, and white-tiled counter fronts. The white interior color scheme conformed to the contemporary notions of cleanliness and hygiene promoted by the City Beautiful movement.

7-046. Interior, Washington Market, New York, New York. Unidentified photographer, 1917. P&P,NYWTS,Subj/Geog-Markets-Washington Market-Retail. LC-DIG-ppsca-12750.

7-044

7-045

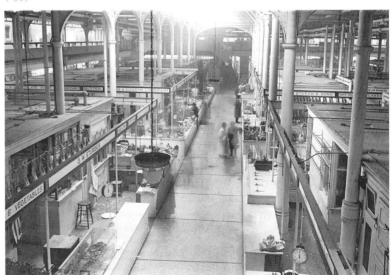

7-046

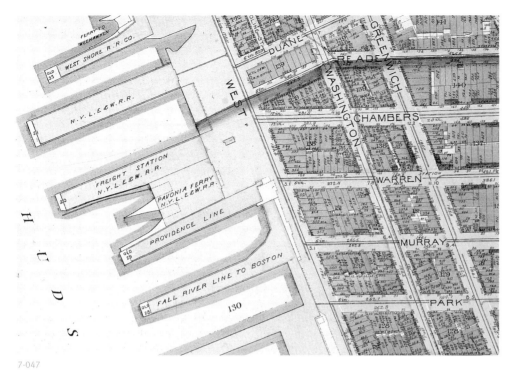

7-047

7-047. Map of the site of Washington Market, New York, New York. From Bromley's *Atlas of the City of New York, Manhattan Island* (1891), plate 2. G&M,G1254.N4 B7 1891,detail(color).

By 1891 the city had reclaimed the landfill on which West Washington Market stood, opposite Washington Market, for steamship docks. West Washington Market was relocated further north to Gansevoort Street (7-048).

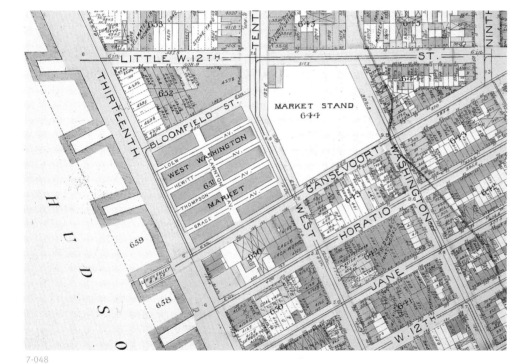

7-048

7-048. Map of the site of West Washington Market, at Gansevoort Street, New York, New York. From Bromley's *Atlas of the City of New York, Manhattan Island* (1891), plate 10. G&M,G1254.N4 B7 1891,detail(color).

West Washington Market was moved from its original site opposite Washington Market to this location (now the site of Piers 52 and 53), in order to be near the large open space for farmers' wagons.

7-049. Washington Market, New York, New York. Al Aumuller, photographer, 1940. P&P,NYWTS,Subj/Geog-Markets-Washington Market-Retail. LC-DIG-ppmsca-12745.

7-050. Washington Wholesale Produce Market, New York, New York. Walter Albertin, photographer, 1952. P&P,NYWTS,Subj/Geog-Markets-Washington Wholesale. LC-DIG-ppmsca-12725.

Washington Market also included rows of wholesale stores that developed northward beginning at the retail market building and extending up to Gansevoort Street.

7-051. Washington Wholesale Produce Market, New York, New York. Al Ravenna, photographer, 1946. P&P,NYWTS,Subj/Geog-Markets-Washington Wholesale. LC-DIG-ppmsca-12726.

7-049

7-050

7-051

7-052

7-053

7-054

7-052. Washington Wholesale Produce Market, New York, New York. Unidentified photographer, 1956. Corbis. P&P,NYWTS,Subj/Geog-Markets-Washington Wholesale. LC-DIG-ppmsca-12729.

7-053. Looking south on Harrison Street, Washington Wholesale Produce Market, New York, New York. Phil Stanziola, photographer, 1968. P&P,NYWTS,Subj/Geog-Markets-Washington Wholesale. LC-DIG-ppmsca-12728.

7-054. Commission merchants, Washington Wholesale Produce Market, New York, New York. Arthur Rothstein, photographer, 1939. P&P,FSA/OWI,LC-USF34- 027130-D.

7-055. Market in lower Manhattan, New York. Samuel H. Gottscho, photographer, before 1934. P&P,LC-G623-T-00205.

7-056. Market in lower Manhattan, New York. Samuel H. Gottscho, photographer, before 1934. P&P,LC-G623-T-00208.

7-057. Market in lower Manhattan, New York. Samuel H. Gottscho, photographer, before 1934. P&P,LC-G623-T-00210.

7-058. Market in lower Manhattan, New York. Samuel H. Gottscho, photographer, before 1934. P&P,LC-G623-T-00209.

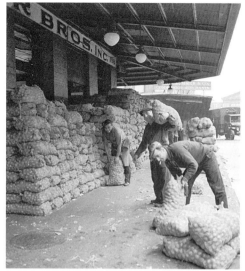

7-055

7-056

7-057

7-058

7-059

7-059. Keeping warm, Washington Wholesale Produce Market, New York, New York. Al Ravenna, photographer, 1950. P&P,NYWTS,Subj/Geog-Markets-Washington Wholesale. LC-DIG-ppmsca-12724.

7-060

7-060. Architect's rendering, Washington Market, New York, New York. New York Department of Public Works, 1940. Al Aumuller, photographer. P&P,NYWTS,Subj/Geog-Markets-Washington Market-Retail. LC-DIG-ppmsca-12749.

The 1884 market house received a facelift in 1940–1941 under the direction of the Department of Public Works and with labor supplied by the Works Progress Administration. The principal structure remained intact and was covered with cinder block faced with enameled metal panels.

7-061. Washington Market, New York, New York. Unidentified photographer, 1941. P&P,NYWTS,Subj/Geog-Markets-Washington Market-Retail. LC-DIG-ppmsca-12741.

A modern aesthetic also was achieved by the addition of a bold, large-scale sign, small display windows, and sidewalks clear of awnings and stands—features that were reminiscent of contemporary department store design.

7-062. Washington Market, New York, New York, taken from Fulton and Washington streets, looking north. Fred Palumbo, photographer, December 29, 1956. P&P,NYWTS,Subj/Geog-Markets-Washington Market-Retail. LC-DIG-ppmsca-12742.

Photo caption reads, "Monday will mark the end of the 144-year history of Washington Market. The downtown retail market has been doomed because it is costing the city $137,000 a year."

7-061

7-062

7-063

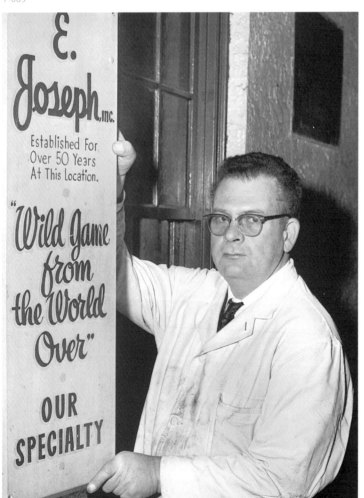

7-064

7-063. Peter's Bar, Washington Market, New York, New York.
Unidentified photographer, 1950. Al Aumuller, photographer.
P&P,NYWTS,Subj/Geog-Markets-Washington Market-Retail. LC-DIG-ppm-sca-12746.

7-064. Milton Joseph Jr., vendor in wild game, Washington Market, New
York, New York. Herman Hiller, photographer, 1957.
P&P,NYWTS,Subj/Geog-Markets-Washington Market-Retail. LC-DIG-ppm-sca-12740.

Washington Market was known among epicures as the great game center of New York. Milton Joseph Jr. presides over the business that his
father established in the 1890s. The stand featured everything from
reindeer meat from Alaska and colored birds from the Far East, to wild
turkeys from Wisconsin and pheasants from New Jersey.

7-065. Washington Market being demolished, New York, New York. Walter Albertin, photographer, 1960. P&P,NYWTS,Subj/Geog-Markets-Washington Market-Retail. LC-DIG-ppmsca-12747.

Dover Management bought Washington Market at auction and hired Associated Wreckers, Inc., for the demolition.

7-066. Sign proclaiming auction of Washington Market, New York, New York, on Monday, December 15, 1958. Walter Albertin, photographer, 1958. P&P,NYWTS,Subj/Geog-Markets-Washington Market-Retail. LC-DIG-ppmsca-12748.

Several attempts to sell the market failed, including this one in 1958. Finally, on September 18, 1959, the Brooklyn firm of Dover Management purchased the entire block, including the market, for $1,106,000.

7-065

7-066

WHOLESALE TERMINAL MARKETS

In the early decades of the twentieth century, federal, state and local governments began to collaborate in the design and construction of new buildings and spaces for large-scale storage and regional distribution of food. These facilities, known as wholesale terminal markets, unified the arrival of food by rail, water, and roads. They also facilitated the distribution of food away from the market—namely, to the various retail outlets throughout the city and region.

The concept of a wholesale terminal market was not new in the twentieth century. One could conceivably look to the granaries and entrepôts of ancient Greece or Rome to find precedents for food warehouses and distribution centers controlled by a public authority. More recently, in the nineteenth century, many European nations shared a concern that conflicts over the food supply might threaten the public order. The high cost of living was a source of widespread discontent and was often a central theme of riots, strikes, and worker protests. Moreover, the growth of armies, civilian employees, and national and provincial capitals fueled a demand for food services and supplies. Government-controlled central markets, therefore, were considered essential for maintaining physical and financial control of the food supply–an important element in the state-making process.

The wholesale terminal market was conceived as a public necessity by government authorities, city planners, and consumers in the United States in the 1910s. The desire for large-scale, planned food storage and distribution centers was driven by high food prices, a fear that food shortages might cause unrest among the foreign-born masses, and ultimately the war among cities for larger markets. These factors rallied popular support for the construction of unified food marketing and distribution centers in the American metropolis. The wholesale terminal market was conceived as a model public market for the twentieth century, and it remains the principal building type dedicated to wholesale food marketing and distribution.

Wholesale terminal markets are located in the business or semi-industrial sections of cities to accommodate railroad and truck deliveries, without confronting city traffic and at a point convenient to buyers. The basic plan of a wholesale terminal market was based upon years of experience moving goods in and out of narrow, deep stores horizontally lining two sides of a wide street in the city center. The principal structure of the complex, therefore, is the long and narrow row of wholesalers' stores, with front and back platforms for transferring loads. Other structures on the site may include an administration building for housing market officials, restaurants, retail stores, and other business activities catering to the public. The complex might also include a produce shed, packing plant, auction house, cold storage plant, slaughterhouse, or cannery.

8-001

8-001. Terminal Market, Munich, Germany. From Mrs. Elmer Black, *A Terminal Market System: New York's Most Urgent Need* (1912), p. 20. Gen. Coll.,HF5470.B5. LC-DIG-ppmsca-12655.

City architect Richard Schachner (1873–1936) designed four parallel market halls in reinforced concrete with cast-iron interior supports. Each market hall specialized in the sale of certain kinds of produce, which arrived by sidings connected to the city's south railway station. Underground cellars were fitted with hydraulic lifts and electric lighting, and the entire complex had a toll department, post office, restaurant, and beer garden. Black described the market as the best equipped in the world.

8-002. East Water Street, Commission Houses, Chicago, Illinois.
T. W. Ingersoll, photographer, 1898. P&P,LC-USZ62-78621.

8-003. Dock Street, Philadelphia, Pennsylvania. Unidentified
photographer, 1908. P&P,DETR,LC-D401-70248.

Dock Street was a principal route with access to the Delaware
River. Its abrupt turn between South Second and Front streets
slowed the flow of traffic and generated constant complaints.
Nonetheless, Dock Street was the site of choice for many commis-
sion houses, freight stations, and wholesale markets, such as the
Delaware Avenue Market.

8-002

8-003

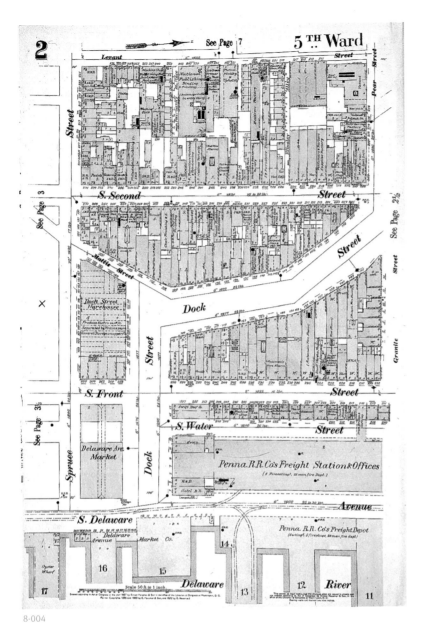

8-004

8-004. Map of Dock Street and the Delaware Avenue Market, Philadelphia, Pennsylvania. From *Insurance Maps of the City of Philadelphia* (Hexamer, 1895), plate 2.
G&M,G1264,P5H,v.1,1895–1898 fol. detail.

8-005. Trucks in the wholesale district, Omaha, Nebraska. John Vachon, photographer, 1938. P&P,FSA/OWI,LC-USF34-008884-D.

8-005

8-006. Light Street looking north, Baltimore, Maryland. Unidentified photographer, 1906. P&P,DETR,LC-USZ62-86647.

One of Baltimore's principal thoroughfares is crowded with market wagons making their way to and from the wholesale stores that flanked the waterfront.

8-007. Wholesale Fish Market, Baltimore, Maryland. Simonson & Pietsch, architects. From *Inland Architect and News Record 50* (September 1907): 36. Gen. Coll.,NA1.15. LC-DIG-ppmsca-12678.

The Great Fire of 1904 demolished 140 acres in the heart of downtown Baltimore, including the city's principal wholesale market known as the Marsh Market. *Inland Architect* described the site before the fire as a complex of "flimsy, delapidated market buildings . . . hemmed in with low, squalid and congested houses—the usual setting for every crime on the court calendar." The new wholesale fish market was brick with terra cotta trim. Inside were twenty-six merchant stalls on the ground floor, with twenty-six corresponding offices on the floor above. The offices opened onto galleries overlooking a vast hall lighted by skylights and great archways at either end of the building. Shipping and receiving were conducted in the rear of the stalls, which were fitted with rolling steel doors opening on to the street.

8-008. Wholesale Produce Market, Baltimore, Maryland. Simonson & Pietsch, architects. From *Inland Architect and News Record 50* (September 1907): 36. Gen. Coll.,NA1.15. LC-DIG-ppmsca-12677.

South of the Wholesale Fish Market (8-018) stood the new wholesale produce market, designed along similar lines in brick and terra cotta trim. This building, measuring approximately 40 by 220 feet, functioned as a great sheltering vestibule for teams of market wagons. The second floor held offices for the city street cleaning department. Design priorities were given to shelter and easy circulation for the greatest number of vehicles and pedestrians. Steel sheds, painted in two shades of green, were erected in the rear plaza to protect pedestrians and drivers; goods were sold directly from wagons.

8-006

8-007

8-008

8-009

8-010

8-011

8-009. Centre (Marsh) Market, Baltimore, Maryland. Unidentified photographer, ca. 1890–1910. P&P,U.S. Geog File-Maryland-Baltimore-Centre Vegetable Market. LC-DIG-ppmsca-12326.

This view shows the wholesale fish and produce markets adjacent to each other, at right, with the produce market in the foreground. In 1976 Baltimore City relocated the wholesale markets to a new $5.6 million wholesale terminal market in Jessup, Maryland—10 miles south of the city. The Centre Market buildings were demolished, with the exception of the facade of the wholesale fish market.

8-010. Opening, showing the new tracks for freight cars, Wallabout Market, Brooklyn, New York, New York. Unidentified photographer, 1936. P&P,NYWTS,Subj/Geog Markets-Wallabout-Brooklyn. LC-DIG-ppmsca-12737.

Wallabout Market opened in 1884 on land that the U.S. Navy leased to the city of Brooklyn. The federal government eventually sold a total of 45 acres to the city, and by the 1890s, Wallabout became one of the world's largest wholesale markets for fruits and vegetables, most of which came from Long Island. The market was expanded in the 1930s during the administration of Mayor Fiorello La Guardia.

8-011. Wallabout Market, Brooklyn, New York, New York. Al Aumuller, photographer, 1940. P&P,NYWTS,Subj/Geog Markets-Wallabout-Brooklyn. LC-DIG-ppmsca-12738.

8-012. Union Produce Terminal, Detroit, Michigan. Unidentified photographer, ca. 1925. AM,Harvard University Graduate School of Design,GSD lantern slide 31518118362. Courtesy of the Frances Loeb Library, Harvard Graduate School of Design.

This market was built on a 38-acre site 4 miles from the Detroit City Hall, at Fort and Green streets. It contained 10 miles of track, and its two main buildings provided 100,000 square feet of sales space.

8-013. Blueprint for a proposed Union Produce Exchange, Chicago, Illinois. Theodore Ahlborn, architect, 1921.LC-DIG-ppmsca-12835.

This design, probably backed by the railroads, would consolidate the receipt of produce arriving by water and rail at a single location. It coincided with the city's plan to build a municipal wholesale terminal market, designed to remove the wholesale trade from the city's principal streets (8-012). These efforts led to the establishment of the Chicago Wholesale Produce Market, a cooperative venture of the commission merchants from the old South Water Street Market (8-027).

8-012

8-013

8-014

8-015

8-016

this is the **MARKET** where the
storekeeper buys the food and brings
it to his store near your house

8-017

8-014. Los Angeles Wholesale Terminal Market, 1396 E. Seventh
Street, Los Angeles, California. John Parkinson, architect. From
Arthur Goodwin, *Markets: Public and Private* (1929), p. 132. Gen.
Coll.,HF5470.G6. LC-DIG-ppmsca-12865.

This market, also known as the Union Wholesale Terminal, was
built in 1917–1918 under the guidance of the Bureau of
Agricultural Economics of the USDA, which had a field office onsite.

8-015. Los Angeles Wholesale Terminal Market, Los Angeles,
California. From Arthur Goodwin, *Markets: Public and Private*
(1929), p. 112. LC-DIG-ppmsca-12864.

8-016. Chicago Wholesale Produce Market, Chicago, Illinois. John
Vachon, photographer, 1941. P&P,FSA/OWI,LC-USF34-063118-D.
Gen. Coll.,HF5470.G6.

New in 1925, this $17 million project was privately funded by the
South Water Street commission merchants, who had to relocate
after the city condemned their old facilities in order to build a
boulevard. The series of six buildings were constructed in reinforced concrete, the preferred material for wholesale terminal
markets, and contained 166 stores, measuring 24 by 80 feet.

8-017. Poster about wholesale food markets. New York: Federal
Art Project, 1936 or 1937. P&P,LC-USZC2-999(color).

8-018. Chicago Wholesale Produce Market, Chicago, Illinois. John Vachon, photographer, 1941. P&P,FSA/OWI,LC-USF34-063021-D.

8-019. Commission merchant supervising unloading of truck, Chicago Wholesale Produce Market, Chicago, Illinois. John Vachon, photographer, 1941. P&P,FSA/OWI,LC-USF34-063024-D.

8-020. Commission merchant examining fruit, Chicago Wholesale Produce Market, Chicago, Illinois. John Vachon, photographer, 1941. P&P,FSA/OWI,LC-USF34-063196-D.

8-021. Warehouse, Chicago Wholesale Produce Market, Chicago, Illinois. John Vachon, photographer, 1941. P&P,FSA/OWI,LC-USF34-063018-D.

8-018

8-019

8-020

8-021

8-022

8-022. Commission merchants and their agents at fruit auction, Chicago Wholesale Produce Market, Chicago, Illinois. John Vachon, photographer, 1941. P&P,FSA/OWI,LC-USF34-063136-D.

8-023. Commission merchant's truck loaded at Chicago Wholesale Produce Market, Chicago, Illinois. John Vachon, photographer, 1941. P&P,FSA/OWI,LC-USF34-063020-D.

8-024. Onions and potatoes at produce market, where commission merchants sell to retailers. Chicago, Illinois. John Vachon, photographer, 1941. P&P,FSA/OWI,LC-USF34-063034-D.

8-025. Trucks of commission merchants lined up to load fruit bought at auction, Chicago Wholesale Produce Market, Chicago, Illinois. John Vachon, photographer, 1941. P&P,FSA/OWI,LC-USF34-063047-D.

8-023

8-025

8-024

BRONX TERMINAL MARKET

Mayor John F. Hylan laid the cornerstone of the Bronx Terminal Market on October 25, 1924. The market was originally conceived as a comprehensively planned industrial complex located on a 28-acre tract along the Harlem River between 149th and 152nd streets. The first and only building constructed for some time on the site was a wholesale market and cold storage warehouse, built in the Lombard revival style. Its fortified, unadorned exterior reflected the building's practical function as a solid container for the long-term storage of food. The six-story structure was approximately 300 feet square, and each floor contained over 100,000 square feet (8-026).

The first two floors of the main building were intended for wholesale merchant stores, and the remaining four floors were for dry goods, cold storage, and freezer space. The ground floor was equipped with platforms that could accommodate goods arriving by rail or truck. Orders were filled on the second floor of the merchant store, where a viaduct provided an immediate exit for loaded trucks to access major highways and bridges en route to retail outlets (8-027).

Mayor La Guardia secured New Deal support to expand the Bronx Terminal Market in 1935. Two rows of merchant stores were constructed adjacent to the original wholesale market and storage building (8-030–8-031). The new buildings, designed by Albert W. Lewis, Samuel Oxhandler, and John D. Churchill, were intended to make the site more human in scale and more aesthetically appealing—features that were accomplished by exploiting the architectural possibilities of concrete. Each store had cantilevered

8-026

canopies at the front and rear to facilitate loading and unloading during inclement weather. One row of wholesale stores terminated at a triangular building that housed retail stores, a bank, a farmers' hotel, and a restaurant bar and grill. The architects made an effort to link the building and wholesale stores stylistically to the original wholesale market and storage building by repeating the same blind arch detailing, molded this time in concrete, along the parapet wall.

The original wholesale market and storage building was constantly plagued by financial troubles, owing to difficulties in securing long-term leases. During World War II, the city leased it to the federal government for storing supplies for the armed forces. After the war, the city briefly lured new tenants who could benefit from large-scale cold storage, such as the Chateau Martin Wine Company. Eventually, the building was abandoned for decades and then demolished in 2005. The row of merchant stores remains occupied by wholesale dealers specializing in the sale of imported foods, but the entire complex is slated for sale and threatened by plans for redevelopment.

previous page

8-026. Bronx Terminal Market, New York, New York. Unidentified photographer, 1935. P&P,NYWTS,Subj/Geog-Markets-Bronx Terminal Market.

this page

8-027. Cross section of wholesale market and storage building, Bronx Terminal Market, New York, New York. From Arthur E. Goodwin, *Markets: Public and Private* (1929), p. 307. Gen. Coll.,HF5470.G6. LC-DIG-ppmsca-12870.

8-028. Power house, Bronx Terminal Market, New York, New York. Unidentified photographer, 1927. P&P,NYWTS,Subj/Geog-Markets-Bronx Terminal Market. LC-DIG-ppmsca-12769.

A power plant was added to the site in 1927 in order to power the refrigeration equipment and elevators in the main building.

Fig. 105—Cross Section of Bronx Terminal Market, New York.

8-027

8-028

8-029. Bronx Terminal Market, New York, New York. Unidentified photographer, 1935. P&P,NYWTS,Subj/Geog-Markets-Bronx Terminal Market. LC-DIG-ppmsca-12766.

8-030. Bronx Terminal Market, New York, New York. Unidentified photographer, 1935. P&P,NYWTS,Subj/Geog-Markets-Bronx Terminal Market. LC-DIG-ppmsca-12768.

8-031. Bronx Terminal Market, New York, New York. Unidentified photographer, 1935. P&P,NYWTS,Subj/Geog-Markets-Bronx Terminal Market. LC-DIG-ppmsca-12767.

8-029

8-030

8-031

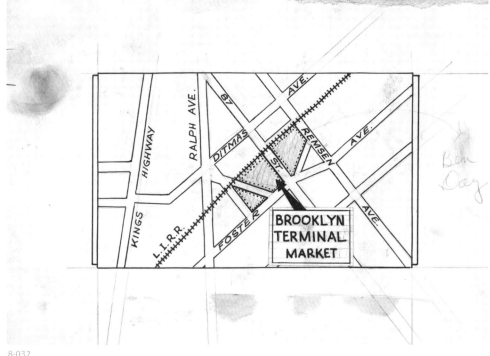

8-032

8-033

8-032. Map, Brooklyn Terminal Market, New York, New York. Department of Markets, City of New York, 1956. P&P,NYWTS,Subj/Geog-Markets-Brooklyn Terminal. LC-DIG-ppm-sca-12754.

8-033. Temporary wooden structures, Brooklyn Terminal Market, New York, New York. Unidentified photographer, 1941. Corbis. P&P,NYWTS,Subj/Geog-Markets-Brooklyn Terminal-Brooklyn,N.Y. LC-DIG-ppmsca-12764.

8-034. Brooklyn Terminal Market, Flatbush, Brooklyn, New York, New York. Gottscho-Schleisner, Inc., 1948. P&P,GSC,LC-G612-T-52624.

8-035. Brooklyn Terminal Market, Flatbush, Brooklyn, New York, New York. Gottscho-Schleisner, Inc., 1948. P&P,GSC,LC-G612-T-52623.

8-036. Canarsie Fruit and Produce Corporation, Brooklyn Terminal Market, New York, New York. Dick De Marsico, photographer, 1962. P&P,NYWTS,Subj/Geog-Markets-Brooklyn Terminal. LC-DIG-ppmsca-12762.

8-034

8-035

8-036

8-037

8-039

8-038

8-037. Eugene Smallwood, weigher at Curatola Banana Corporation, Brooklyn Terminal Market, New York, New York. Dick De Marsico, photographer, 1962. P&P,NYWTS,Subj/Geog-Markets-Brooklyn Terminal. LC-DIG-ppmsca-12758.

8-038. Stanley Hyams, Washington Pickle Works, Brooklyn Terminal Market, New York, New York. Roger Higgins, photographer, 1959. P&P,NYWTS,Subj/Geog-Markets-Brooklyn Terminal. LC-DIG-ppmsca-12757.

8-039. Sy Bayman, Brooklyn Terminal Market, New York, New York. Dick De Marsico, photographer, 1962. P&P,NYWTS,Subj/Geog-Markets-Brooklyn Terminal. LC-DIG-ppmsca-12760.

8-040. Anthony Nocella holds a 110-pound provolone cheese, Brooklyn Terminal Market, New York, New York. Roger Higgins, photographer, 1959. P&P,NYWTS,Subj/Geog-Markets-Brooklyn Terminal. LC-DIG-ppmsca-12761.

8-041. Sorting tomatoes, Iris Fruit Corporation, Brooklyn Terminal Market, New York, New York. Dick De Marsico, photographer, 1962. P&P,NYWTS,Subj/Geog-Markets-Brooklyn Terminal. LC-DIG-ppmsca-12763.

8-042. Fruit and vegetable market, Brooklyn Terminal Market, New York, New York. Walter Albertin, photographer, 1951. P&P,NYWTS,Subj/Geog-Markets-Brooklyn Terminal. LC-DIG-ppmsca-12759.

8-041

8-040

8-042

8-043

8-044

8-043. Watermelon Day, 1964, Brooklyn Terminal Market, New York, New York. Phyllis Twachtman, photographer. P&P,NYWTS,Subj/Geog-Markets-Brooklyn Terminal. LC-DIG-ppmsca-12756.

8-044. Architectural rendering, New Meat Center at Brooklyn Terminal Market, New York, New York. Department of Markets, City of New York, 1961. P&P,NYWTS,Subj/Geog-Markets-Brooklyn Terminal. LC-DIG-ppmsca-12765.

8-045. A scene in a wholesale meat market. A reconstruction photographed during the filming of *Black Marketing*, a motion picture produced by the U.S. Office of War Information (OWI). Roger Smith, photographer, 1943. P&P,FSA/OWI,LC-USW3-030807-C.

8-046. Architectural rendering, Gansevoort Market, New York, New York. Alexander D. Grosett & Associates, architects and engineers. Department of Public Works, City of New York, 1949. P&P,NYWTS,Subj/Geog-Markets-Gansevoort Market,Brooklyn. LC-DIG-ppmsca-12751.

8-045

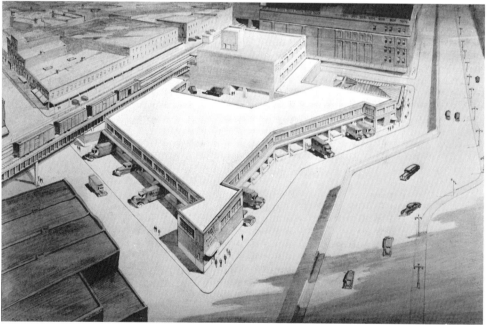

8-046

8-047

8-048

8-049

8-047. Ground breaking, New York City Terminal Market, Hunt's Point, The Bronx, New York, New York. Al Ravenna, photographer, 1962. P&P,NYWTS,Subj/Geog-Markets-Hunt's Point Market. LC-DIG-ppmsca-12698.

8-048. Architectural rendering, New York City Terminal Market, Hunt's Point, The Bronx, New York, New York. Skidmore, Owings & Merrill, architects. Department of Markets, City of New York, 1966. P&P,NYWTS,Subj/Geog-Markets-Hunt's Point Market. LC-DIG-ppmsca-12700.

8-049. Sidetracks, New York City Terminal Market, Hunt's Point, The Bronx, New York, New York. Nat Fein, photographer, 1967. P&P,NYWTS,Subj/Geog-Markets-Hunt's Point Market. LC-DIG-ppmsca-12705.

8-050. Truck loading, New York City Terminal Market, Hunt's Point, The Bronx, New York, New York. Nat Fein, photographer, 1967. P&P,NYWTS,Subj/Geog-Markets-Hunt's Point Market. LC-DIG-ppmsca-12704.

8-051. First National Bank, New York City Terminal Market, Hunt's Point, The Bronx, New York, New York. Nat Fein, photographer, 1967. P&P,NYWTS,Subj/Geog-Markets-Hunt's Point Market. LC-DIG-ppmsca-12703.

8-052. Barber shop, New York City Terminal Market, Hunt's Point, The Bronx, New York, New York. Nat Fein, photographer, 1967. P&P,NYWTS,Subj/Geog-Markets-Hunt's Point Market. LC-DIG-ppmsca-12701.

8-053. Cocktail bar and restaurant, New York City Terminal Market, Hunt's Point, The Bronx, New York, New York. Nat Fein, photographer, 1967. P&P,NYWTS,Subj/Geog-Markets-Hunt's Point Market. LC-DIG-ppmsca-12702.

8-050

8-051

8-052

8-053

FULTON FISH MARKET

The Fulton Fish Market is the oldest and one of the largest wholesale fish markets in the United States. It was located along the East River in lower Manhattan from 1820, when a few fish stalls began to operate in Fulton Market—a general market for all types of food (9-001). Natural features, including deep waters and rapid currents, made Fulton Market particularly favorable for fish sales, eventually leading to separate quarters for a fish market at the head of the slip, opposite the main market, in the 1830s (9-005).

The wholesale trade prospered at Fulton Fish Market in the 1850s, owing to the Long Island Railroad, good water and slip accommodations, and a new bulkhead constructed in 1850. The building was basically a wooden shed that ran the length of the bulkhead from dock to dock. The rear of the shed extended out over the basin, where fishermen could unload their catch directly from their boats into railroad car floats.

Fulton Fish Market remained essentially unchanged for the next 120 years, with the exception of the physical plant. In 1860 a more permanent building replaced the old wooden shed (9-006–9-007), and in 1910 another building was added to the site (9-008–9-010). The latter building collapsed in 1936 (9-012) and was replaced in 1939 with another building during the administration of Mayor Fiorello La Guardia (9-015–9-016).

In the late 1970s, fishing boats ceased landing their catches at the market, having been superceded by refrigerated trucks as the principal means of delivery. The market continued to provide fresh fish from all over the continent and overseas to restaurants, hotels, and retail stores around the New York metropolitan area. Rather than modernize the facilities, the city decided to move Fulton Fish Market in order to use the land for more profitable purposes. In 2005 the market was relocated to a new 400,000-square-foot facility at Hunt's Point in the Bronx, marking the end of one of the last working areas of the Manhattan waterfront.

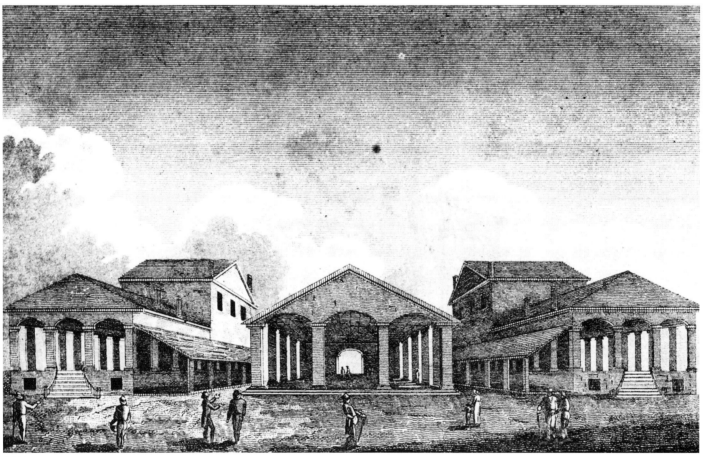

9-001

9-001. *Fulton Market*, New York. New York. Balch, Rawdon & Company, engravers, ca. 1820. P&P,NYWTS,Subj/Geog-Markets-Fulton Fish Market,folder 1 of 2. LC-DIG-ppmsca-12770.

9-002

9-004

9-003

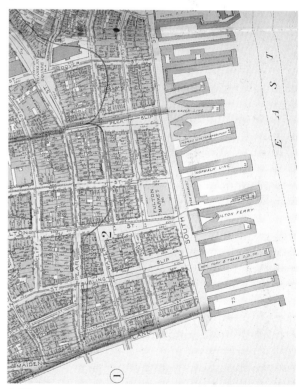

9-005

9-002. Oyster stalls and lunch rooms at Fulton Market, New York, New York. From *Frank Leslie's Illustrated Newspaper* 24, no. 607 (May 18, 1867): 136. P&P,LC-USZ62-128743.

9-003. Oyster stands in Fulton Market, New York, New York. From *Harper's Weekly* 14, no. 722 (October 29, 1870): 701. P&P,LC-USZ62-128025.

9-004. Architectural detail, Fulton Market, New York, New York. Unidentified photographer, 1939. P&P,NYWTS,Subj/Geog-Markets-Fulton Fish Market,folder 2 of 2. LC-DIG-ppmsca-12801.

9-005. Map of the site of Fulton Market and Fulton Fish Market, New York, New York. From *Atlas of the City of New York, Manhattan Island* (Bromley, 1891), plate 3. G&M,G1254.N4 B7 1891,detail(color).

9-006

9-007

9-008

9-006. *New Fish Market, New York City*. Engraving, after sketch by Theo. R. Davis, after 1869. P&P,NYWTS,Subj/Geog-Markets-Fulton Fish Market,folder 1 of 2. LC-DIG-ppmsca-12773.

9-007. Fulton Fish Market, New York, New York. Fred Palumbo, photographer, 1951. P&P,NYWTS,Subj/Geog-Markets-Fulton Fish Market,folder 2 of 2. LC-DIG-ppmsca-12798.

9-008. Fulton Fish Market, New York, New York. From *American Architect and Building News* 97 (March 23, 1910): pt. 1, n. 1787. MMRC,Microfilm 05422,no. 629,detail.

The new wholesale fish market, at the foot of Beekman Street, East River, was designed by Walker & Hazzard and opened for business in 1910. The building was steel reinforced concrete, with ornamental copper detailing on the exterior. It was divided into fifteen stores of equal dimension, each with its own gangway leading to the water on the first floor. Two mezzanine stories were devoted to private offices, toilets, and lockers for employees. The top story had a storeroom extending the entire length of the building, lighted by central skylights and end windows.

9-009

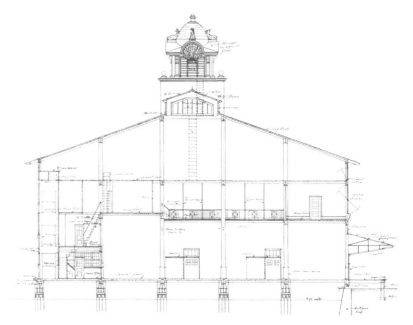

9-010

9-011

9-009. Fulton Fish Market, New York, New York. Unidentified photographer, before 1936. P&P, LC-USZ62-74688.

9-010. Elevation, Fulton Fish Market, New York, New York. From *American Architect and Building News* 97 (March 23, 1910): pt. 1, no. 1787. MMRC, Microfilm 05422, no. 629, detail.

The problem confronting the architects was to construct a light building, extending out over the water, with a steel frame protected by rust from nearby salt water. The building rested on piles of yellow pine timber at the high-water mark.

9-011. Fulton Fish Market, New York, New York. Unidentified photographer, ca. 1910–1940. P&P, LC-USZ62-113344.

9-012

9-013

9-014

9-015

9-012. Fulton Market slides into river when 25-year-old piles give way, New York, New York. Unidentified photographer, 1936. P&P,NYWTS,Subj/Geog-Markets-Fulton Fish Market,folder 1 of 2. LC-DIG-ppmsca-12778.

9-013. Fulton Fish Market, New York, New York. Gordon Parks, photographer, 1943. P&P,FSA/OWI,LC-USW3-028727-E.

9-014. Fulton Fish Market, New York, New York. Dick De Marsico, photographer, 1963. P&P,NYWTS,Subj/Geog-Markets-Fulton Fish Market,folder 1 of 2. LC-DIG-ppmsca-12774.

9-015. Mayor Fiorello La Guardia poses with a 300-pound halibut at the dedication of the new Fulton Fish Market, New York, New York. C.M. Stieglitz, photographer, 1939. P&P,NYWTS,Subj/Geog-Markets-Fulton Fish Market,folder 1 of 2. LC-DIG-ppmsca-12771.

9-016

9-016. Fulton Fish Market, New York, New
York. Dick De Marsico, photographer, 1963.
P&P,NYWTS,Subj/Geog-Markets-Fulton Fish
Market,folder 2 of 2. LC-DIG-ppmsca-12787.

9-017

9-018

9-019

9-017. Scene on a trawler off the Georges Banks. Unidentified photographer, 1939. P&P,NYWTS,Subj/Geog-Markets-Fulton Fish Market,folder 1 of 2. LC-DIG-ppmsca-12783.

The fish are caught, cleaned, and put into refrigeration within a few minutes. They come to the dock ready for marketing.

9-018. Fulton Fish Market, New York, New York. Unidentified photographer, 1939. LC-DIG-ppmsca-127750.

9-019. Captain William Dennis, of Port Monmouth, New Jersey, unloads fish from his freight boat *Edith*, Fulton Fish Market, New York, New York. Fred Palumbo, photographer, 1943. P&P,NYWTS,Subj/Geog-Markets-Fulton Fish Market,folder 2 of 2. LC-DIG-ppmsca-12799.

9-020

9-021

9-020. Dock stevedores at the Fulton Fish Market, New York, New York. Gordon Parks, photographer, 1943. P&P,FSA/OWI,LC-USW3-024043-E.

The stevedores are sending up baskets of fish from the holds of the boats to the docks where it is bought, stored in barrels, and packed in ice for delivery to wholesalers.

9-021. Stevedores unloading fish caught off the New England coast, Fulton Fish Market, New York, New York. Gordon Parks, photographer, 1943. P&P,FSA/OWI,LC-USW3-024018-E.

9-022. Weighing fish unloaded from dragger *Nautilus*, using scoop scales, Fulton Fish Market, New York, New York. Fred Palumbo, photographer, ca. 1950. P&P,NYWTS,Subj/Geog-Markets-Fulton Fish Market,folder 2 of 2. LC-DIG-ppmsca-12795.

9-023. Weighing mackerel, Fulton Fish Market, New York, New York. Unidentified photographer, 1934. P&P,NYWTS,Subj/Geog-Markets-Fulton Fish Market,folder 1 of 2. LC-DIG-ppmsca-12784.

9-022

9-023

9-024

9-025

9-027

9-026

9-024. *Weighing Fish*. Wood engraving by M. Lois Murphy, 1936 or 1937. P&P,LC-USZC4-6584.

9-025. Hooker shoveling redfish onto the scales in the Fulton Fish Market, New York, New York. Gordon Parks, photographer, 1943. P&P,FSA/OWI,LC-USW3-028749-D.

9-026. Buck Steo weighs fresh load of mackerel, Fulton Fish Market, New York, New York. Fred Palumbo, photographer, 1938. P&P,NYWTS,Subj/Geog-Markets-Fulton Fish Market,folder 2 of 2. LC-DIG-ppmsca-12800.

9-027. Dock stevedores unloading and weighing fish in the early morning, Fulton Fish Market, New York, New York. Gordon Parks, photographer, 1943. P&P,FSA/OWI,LC-USW3-024103-E.

9-028. James Polito, Nick Russo, and Jack La Fanci weighing fish, Fulton Fish Market, New York, New York. Fred Palumbo, photographer, 1951. P&P,NYWTS,Subj/Geog-Markets-Fulton Fish Market,folder 2 of 2. LC-DIG-ppmsca-12797.

9-029. Jimmy Liebl, salesman, shouts code message to bookkeeper in back after a sale of lobsters is made, Eastern Commission Company, Fulton Fish Market, New York, New York. Unidentified photographer, 1939. P&P,NYWTS,Subj/Geog-Markets-Fulton Fish Market,folder 1 of 2. LC-DIG-ppmsca-12782.

9-030. Weighing fish, Fulton Fish Market, New York, New York. Unidentified photographer, 1952. P&P,NYWTS,Subj/Geog-Markets-Fulton Fish Market,folder 1 of 2. LC-DIG-ppmsca-12777.

9-031. Weighing fish, Fulton Fish Market, New York, New York. Dick De Marsico, photographer, 1963. P&P,NYWTS,Subj/Geog-Markets-Fulton Fish Market,folder 2 of 2. LC-DIG-ppmsca-12796.

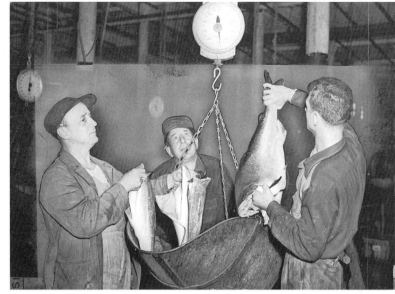

9-028

9-029

9-030

9-031

9-032

9-033

9-034

9-035

9-032. Stevedore, Fulton Fish Market, New York, New York. Gordon Parks, photographer, 1943. P&P,FSA/OWI,LC-USW3-024125-E.

9-033. Hooker, Fulton Fish Market, New York, New York. Gordon Parks, photographer, 1943. P&P,FSA/OWI,LC-USW3-031326-E.

9-034. Hooker, Fulton Fish Market, New York, New York. Gordon Parks, photographer, 1943. P&P,FSA/OWI,LC-USW3-031327-E.

9-035. Dock stevedore holding giant lobster claws, Fulton Fish Market, New York, New York. Gordon Parks, photographer, 1943. P&P,FSA/OWI,LC-USW3-024014-E.

9-036. Interior, Fulton Fish Market, New York, New York. Walter Albertin, photographer, 1954. P&P,NYWTS,Subj/Geog-Markets-Fulton Fish Market,folder 1 of 2. LC-DIG-ppmsca-12772.

9-036

9-037. Fisherman holding a large catch at the Fulton Fish Market, New York, New York. Gordon Parks, photographer, 1943. P&P,FSA/OWI,LC-USW3-028719-E.

9-038. Gloucester fishermen resting on their boat, Fulton Fish Market, New York, New York. Gordon Parks, photographer, 1943. P&P,FSA/OWI,LC-USW3-024065-E.

9-039. Sal Leggio with striped bass, Fulton Fish Market, New York, New York. Orlando Fernandez, photographer, 1962. P&P,NYWTS,Subj/Geog-Markets-Fulton Fish Market,folder 1 of 2. LC-DIG-ppmsca-12779.

9-037

9-038

9-039

9-040

9-041

9-040. Glouchester fishermen resting in
their bunks after unloading their catch,
Fulton Fish Market, New York, New York.
Gordon Parks, photographer, 1943.
P&P,FSA/OWI,LC-USW3-028740-D.

9-041. Keeping warm, Fulton Fish Market,
New York, New York. John Bottega, photog-
rapher, 1964. P&P,NYWTS,Subj/Geog-
Markets-Fulton Fish Market,folder 2 of 2. LC-
DIG-ppmsca-12789.

9-042

9-043

9-044

9-042. Plaques listing Fulton Fish Market men in the armed forces, Fulton Fish Market, New York, New York. Gordon Parks, photographer, 1943. P&P,FSA/OWI,LC-USW3-028713-E.

9-043. Dock scene, Fulton Fish Market, New York, New York. Gordon Parks, photographer, 1943. P&P,FSA/OWI,LC-USW3-024051-E.

9-044. A buyer visits the wholesale district to purchase fish for his store, Fulton Fish Market, New York, New York. Gordon Parks, photographer, 1943. P&P,FSA/OWI,LC-USW3-028720-E.

9-045. Fulton Fish Market, New York, New York. Unidentified photographer, 1939. Corbis. P&P,NYWTS,Subj/Geog-Markets-Fulton Fish Market,folder 1 of 2. LC-DIG-ppm-sca-12791.

9-046. Fulton Fish Market, New York, New York. Unidentified photographer, 1946. Corbis. P&P,NYWTS,Subj/Geog-Markets-Fulton Fish Market,folder 2 of 2. LC-DIG-ppm-sca-12786.

9-045

9-046

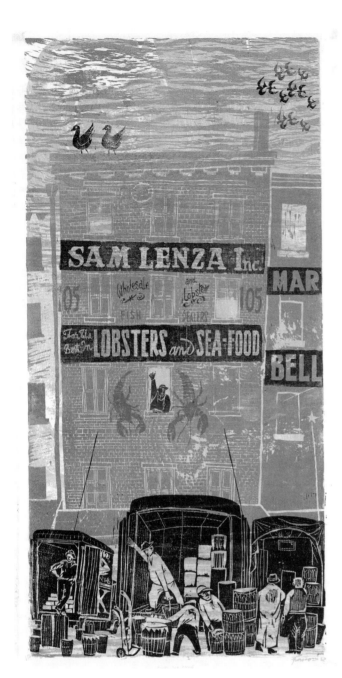

9-047

9-050

9-047. *Fulton Fish Market, New York.* Woodcut by Antonio Frasconi, 1952. P&P,FP-XX-F837,no. 7(C size).

9-048. Shipping fish by horse-drawn vehicle from Fulton Fish Market, New York, New York. Gordon Parks, photographer, 1943. P&P,FSA/OWI,LC-USW3-028731-E.

9-049. Watering fish with brine water, Fulton Fish Market, New York, New York. Gordon Parks, photographer, 1943. P&P,FSA/OWI,LC-USW3-028716-E.

9-050. Pushcart fruit vendor, Fulton Fish Market, New York, New York. Gordon Parks, photographer, 1943. P&P,FSA/OWI,LC-USW3-028760-D.

9-048

9-049

9-051. Barrels of fish on the docks ready to be shipped to retailers and wholesalers, Fulton Fish Market, New York, New York. Gordon Parks, photographer, 1943. P&P, FSA/OWI, LC-USW3-024093-E.

9-052. Barrels of fish on the docks ready to be shipped to retailers, Fulton Fish Market, New York, New York. Gordon Parks, photographer, 1943. P&P,FSA/OWI,LC-USW3-024096-E.

9-053. Ice used to store fish on boats that bring their catches into Fulton Fish Market, New York, New York. Gordon Parks, photographer, 1943. P&P,FSA/OWI, LC-USW3-028746-D.

9-051

9-052

9-053

9-054. Icing barrels of fish, Fulton Fish Market, New York, New York. Gordon Parks, photographer, 1943. P&P, FSA/OWI, LC-USW3-024086-E.

9-055. James Lentini, ice handler, Fulton Fish Market, New York, New York. Ed Ford, photographer, 1959. P&P,NYWTS,Subj/Geog-Markets-Fulton Fish Market,folder 1 of 2. LC-DIG-ppmsca-12776.

9-056. Mrs. Elizabeth Michelin packs haddock at Jim Walsh Fillet Company, Fulton Fish Market, New York, New York. Fred Palumbo, photographer, 1943. P&P,NYWTS,Subj/Geog-Markets-Fulton Fish Market,folder 1 of 2. LC-DIG-ppm-sca-12785.

9-057. Apicella Brothers, mussel kings of Fulton Fish Market, New York, New York. Fred Palumbo, photographer, 1943. LC-DIG-ppmsca-12794.

9-058. Fulton Fish Market, New York, New York. Gordon Parks, photographer, 1943. P&P,FSA/OWI,LC-USW3-024079-E.

9-054

9-055

9-056

9-057

9-058

9-059. Louis De Marco and Michael Tolento dancing with a fish at the Fulton Fish Market, New York, New York. Dick De Marsico, photographer, 1962. P&P,NYWTS,Subj/Geog-Markets-Fulton Fish Market,folder 1 of 2. LC-DIG-ppmsca-12781.

9-060. City sanitation workman washing streets at Fulton Fish Market, New York, New York. Gordon Parks, photographer, 1943. P&P,FSA/OWI,LC-USW3-030288-D.

9-061. Fulton Fish Market, New York. Gordon Parks, photographer, 1943. P&P,FSA/OWI,LC-USW3-030276-D.

9-059

9-060

9-061

MARKET DAY

Market day begins long before the public arrives. Farmers, fishermen, butchers, bakers, and other producers spend the preceding days gathering or preparing their goods; and just "going to market," for some, means making a long journey from the village or countryside to the town. Once at the market, vendors begin to prepare their stalls and stands. During market hours, time is spent waiting for customers or taking a break. Customers arrive with market baskets in hand, comparing prices, judging quality, and making their selections.

Market day is also a busy time for the people whose job it is to manage, inspect, clean, or police the market; others are employed to handle, pack, ship, or transport merchandise. All of these activities, including the actual buying and selling, contribute to making the marketplace an attractive environment for anyone interested in getting the attention of a captive audience. Politicians, for example, are known to frequent markets in an effort to win votes. Likewise, proselytizers, street entertainers, bootblacks, pickpockets, and beggars profit from the crowd.

This section divides market day into the most common activities: going to market, getting ready, waiting, shopping, making a sale, weighing and inspecting, working the crowd, taking a break, and going home.

GOING TO MARKET

10-001

10-001. Four Palestinian women on way to market with baskets on heads. American Colony Photo Department or Matson Photo Service, ca. 1898–1946. P&P,LC-DIG-matpc-07350.

10-002. *Going to Market, Mexico.* Etching by Peter Moran, 1890. P&P,LC-USZ62-106231.

10-003. Sheep and goats being taken to market, Jerusalem, Palestine. Unidentified photographer, ca. 1880–1920. P&P,LC-USZ62-93096.

10-002

10-003

10-004. African men and woman arriving at the monthly wild rubber village market, carrying rubber and supplies, Lebango, Moyen Congo. Brazzaville Bureau, Office of War Information, ca. 1943. P&P,LC-USZ62-130448.

10-005. On the way to market at Mendria, Greece. Lewis Wickes Hine, photographer, 1918. P&P,NCLC,LC-USZ62-90518.

10-004

10-005

10-006

10-007

10-008

10-006. Walking to market, Hungary. Unidentified photographer, 1924. P&P,LC-USZ62-113783.

10-007. *Going to Market—A Scene near Savannah, Georgia.* From *Harper's Weekly* (May 29, 1875): p 436. P&P,LC-USZ62-102153.

10-008. *Floating Down to Market.* Lithograph. Currier & Ives, 1870. P&P,LC-USZC2-2338.

10-009. A young Berger nomad rides into Timbuktu for market day, Timbuktu, Mali. Syndicat d'Initiative du Soudan, ca. 1960–1970. P&P,NYWTS,Subj/Geog-Mali-Timbuktu. LC-DIG-ppm-sca-12753.

10-009

10-010.

10-011.

10-012.

10-013.

10-010. "Mammy going to market." Unidentified photographer, 1902. P&P,DETR,LC-D4-14746.

10-011. Going to market, New Orleans, Louisiana. Arnold Genthe, photographer, ca. 1920–1926. P&P,LC-G406-T-0074.

10-012. Driving boy taking pigs to market, Winchester Vic., Kentucky. Lewis Wickes Hine, photographer, 1916. P&P,NCLC,LC-DIG-nclc-00533.

10-013. Men transporting bananas to the city markets, Panama. Publishers Photo Service, ca. 1890–1923. P&P,LC-USZ62-97799.

10-014

10-015

10-016

10-014. Train of market wagons, Mexico. Unidentified photographer, 1922. P&P,Foreign Geog File-Mexico.

10-015. Truckload of beef being delivered to Center Market, Washington, D.C. National Photo Company Collection, 1923. P&P,LC-USZ62-94998.

10-016. Farmer takes his hay to market near Toledo, Ohio. Alfred T. Palmer, photographer, 1941. P&P,FSA/OWI,LC-USW3-055510-C.

10-017

10-018

10-019

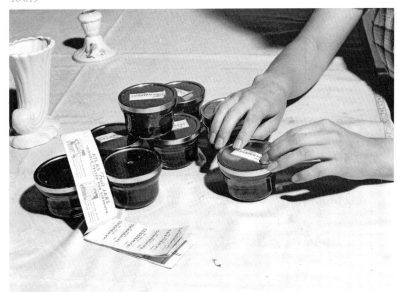

10-020

10-017. Mrs. Merritt Bundy and her daughter picking beans for sale at the Tri-County Farmers Co-operative Market in Du Bois, Pennsylvania, on their farm near Penfield, Pennsylvania. Jack Delano, photographer, 1940. P&P,FSA/OWI,LC-USF34-041366-E.

10-018. Washing eggs to be sold at Tri-County Farmers Co-operative Market at Du Bois, Pennsylvania, on Reitz farm, near Falls Creek, Pennsylvania. Jack Delano, photographer, 1940. P&P,FSA/OWI,LC-USF34-041201-D.

10-019. Preparing tomatoes for sale at the Tri-County Farmers Co-operative Market at Du Bois, Pennsylvania, on the farm of Mr. Kness near Penfield, Pennsylvania. Jack Delano, photographer, 1940. P&P,FSA/OWI,LC-USF34-041249-D.

10-020. Pasting labels on strawberry jelly to be sold at Tri-County Farmers Co-operative Market at Du Bois, Pennsylvania, on the Reitz's farm, near Falls Creek, Pennsylvania. Jack Delano, photographer, 1940. P&P,FSA/OWI,LC-USF34-041198-D.

10-021. The booth of Mr. Kness at the Tri-County Farmers Co-operative Market in Du Bois, Pennsylvania. Jack Delano, photographer, 1940. P&P,FSA/OWI,LC-USF34-041317-D.

10-021

10-022

10-023

10-022. In the public market at Athens, Greece, the animals are killed while you wait. Lewis Wickes Hine, photographer, 1918. P&P,NCLC,LC-USZ62-90525.

10-023. Radish seller, Sixth Street Market, Cincinnati, Ohio. Lewis Wickes Hine, photographer, 1908. P&P,LC-DIG-nclc-03199.

10-024. Visions of sauerkraut, Germany. Carleton H. Graves, publisher, 1900. P&P,LC-USZ62-112663.

10-024

10-025

10-026

10-025. Young chicken vendors, Sixth Street Market, Cincinnati, Ohio. Lewis Wickes Hine, photographer, 1908. P&P,NCLC,LC-DIG-nclc-03190.

10-026. Market vendors, Wilmington, Delaware. Lewis Wickes Hine, photographer, 1910. P&P,NCLC,LC-DIG-nclc-03568.

10-027. Scene in farmer's market, Weatherford, Texas. Russell Lee, photographer, 1939. P&P,FSA/OWI,LC-USF331-012281-M1.

10-027

10-028

10-029

10-028. *At the Market, Richmond, Virginia.* Wood engraving by William Ludwell Sheppard, 1868. P&P, LC-USZ62-111074.

10-029. U.S. Secretary of Agriculture Henry C. Wallace and his wife shopping at Center Market, Washington, D.C. Unidentified photographer, ca. 1921–1924. P&P, LC-USZ62-92860.

10-030. African Americans at sheltered outdoor market or fair. W.E.B. Du Bois, collector, 1899 or 1900. P&P, LC-USZ62-124845.

10-031. Woman selling food in a market, Hungary. Unidentified photographer, ca. 1920–1923. P&P, LC-USZ62-113800.

10-030

10-031

10-032

10-033

10-032. Young vendor at King Street Market, Wilmington, Delaware. Lewis Wickes Hine, photographer, 1910. P&P,NCLC,LC-DIG-nclc-03571.

10-033. Customers entering Tri-County Farmers Co-operative Market in Du Bois, Pennsylvania. Jack Delano, photographer, 1940. P&P,FSA/OWI,LC-USF34-041315-D.

10-034. Vegetable market, Rome, Italy. Leo Stoecker, photographer, 1946. Leo Stoecker/Corbis. P&P,NYWTS,Subj/Geog-Italy-Rome-Markets. LC-DIG-ppmsca-12692.

10-035. Mennonites at the farmers' market, Lititz, Pennsylvania. Marjory Collins, photographer, 1942. P&P,FSA/OWI,LC-USW3-011298-E.

10-034

10-035

10-036. Market scene, Barcelos, Portugal. Bernard Hoffman, photographer, ca. 1920–1947. P&P,AHC,Ac. No. 6125. LC-DIG-ppm-sca-12475.

10-037. Mrs. Ellen Lewin shopping in the Bleecker Street market, New York, New York. Fred Palumbo, photographer, 1962. P&P,NYWTS,Subj/Geog-Markets-Push Cart. LC-DIG-ppmsca-12718.

10-038

10-040

10-039

10-041

10-038. Goats milked while you wait—in a crowded market-place in old Palermo, Sicily. Underwood & Underwood, 1906. P&P,LC-USZ62-73497.

10-039. Mennonite farmer and wife selling fowl at the farmer's market, Lititz, Pennsylvania. Marjory Collins, photographer, 1942. P&P,FSA/OWI,LC-USW3-011292-E.

10-040. Farm family at Tri-County Farmers Co-operative Market at Du Bois, Pennsylvania. Jack Delano, photographer, 1940. P&P,FSA/OWI,LC-USF34-041287-D.

10-041. Inside of the Tri-County Farmers Co-operative Market at Du Bois, Pennsylvania. Jack Delano, photographer, 1940. P&P,FSA/OWI,LC-USF34-041230-D.

10-042. Open air market, Paris, France. Unidentified photographer, 1945. P&P,NYWTS,Subj/Geog-France-Paris-Markets. AP/Wide World Photos. LC-DIG-ppmsca-12804.

10-042

10-043

10-045

10-043. Woman selling vegetables in a market, Hungary. Unidentified photographer, 1923. P&P,LC-USZ62-113791.

10-044. Setting up the scales on a vegetable truck at the early morning market, San Antonio, Texas. Russell Lee, photographer, 1939. P&P,FSA/OWI,LC-USF34-032690-D.

10-045. Young woman street vendor holding measuring scales, India. William Henry Jackson, photographer, 1895. P&P,WTCPC,W7-423(color).

10-046. Lester P. W. (Pete) Wehle, live-poultry inspector, New York City, Department of Markets. Al Ravenna, photographer, 1951. P&P,NYWTS,Subj/Geog-New York City-Markets,Department of. LC-DIG-ppmsca-12730.

10-044

10-046

10-047. A man examining meat in a wholesale meat market. A reconstruction photographed during the filming of *Black Marketing*, a motion picture produced by the U.S. Office of War Information (OWI). Roger Smith, photographer, 1943. P&P,FSA/OWI,LC-USW3-030806-C.

10-048. Matthew A. Donohue, inspector of weights and measures, New York City, Department of Markets. Dick De Marsico, photographer, 1951. P&P,NYWTS,Subj/Geog-New York City-Markets,Department of. LC-DIG-ppmsca-12731.

10-049. Albert S. Pacetta, Commissioner, New York City Department of Markets, smashes scales confiscated by inspectors. Fred Palumbo, photographer, 1960. P&P,NYWTS,Subj/Geog-New York City-Markets,Department of. LC-DIG-ppmsca-12734.

10-048

10-047

10-049

10-050

10-050. William Jay Gaynor, Mayor of New York, at Washington Market, New York City, New York. Unidentified photographer, ca. 1910–1913. P&P,LC-DIG-ggbain-06787.

10-051. Miss Mimi Fellers, Watermelon Queen, from South Carolina and Abe Stark, City Council President, Brooklyn Terminal Market, New York, New York. Al Ravenna, photographer, 1961. P&P,NYWTS,Subj/Geog-Watermelons. LC-DIG-ppmsca-12688.

10-052. Watermelon Day, Brooklyn Terminal Market, New York, New York. Phyllis Twachtman, photographer, 1964. P&P,NYWTS,Subj/Geog-Markets-Brooklyn Terminal. LC-DIG-ppmsca-12755.

10-052

10-051

10-053. Mayor Knapp attends the farmers'
market, located in the heart of downtown
Lexington, Virginia, to buy fresh produce.
Carol Highsmith, photographer, September
29, 2002. P&P,LC-DIG-pplot-13600-
01237(color).

10-053

10-054

10-055

10-056

10-054. Noontime, fish market, Lisbon, Portugal. Unidentified photographer, 1911. P&P,Foreign Geog File,Portugal-Lisbon. LC-DIG-ppmsca-12307.

10-055. Man sleeping in fish market, Baltimore, Maryland. Sheldon Dick, photographer, 1938. P&P,FSA/OWI,LC-USF33-020017-M1.

10-056. Tomato peddler asleep in the back of his truck at early morning vegetable market, San Antonio, Texas. Russell Lee, photographer, 1939. P&P,FSA/OWI,LC-USF34-032658-D.

10-057

10-058

10-057. Cook who works in one of the seafood restaurants in the fish market district, Washington, D.C. John Ferrell, photographer, 1942. P&P,FSA/OWI,LC-USF34-011448-D.

10-058. Wives of vegetable peddlers sometimes accompany their husbands to the early morning market, San Antonio, Texas. Russell Lee, photographer, 1939. P&P,FSA/OWI,LC-USF34-032648-D.

10-059

10-060

10-059. Tony on His Way Home from the Market Bringing Chicken-Heads and Feet to Sell to the Soap Man, Boston, Massachusetts. Lewis Wickes Hine, photographer, 1909. P&P,NCLC,LC-DIG-nclc-04530.

10-060. A boy carrying home decayed refuse from markets, Boston, Massachusetts. Lewis Wickes Hine, photographer, 1909. P&P,NCLC,LC-USZ62-86814.

10-061

10-062

10-061. Customers at the entrance of the Tri-County Farmers Co-operative Market in Du Bois, Pennsylvania. Jack Delano, photographer, 1940. P&P,FSA/OWI,LC-USF34-041390-E.

10-062. Customers' cars parked in front of Tri-County Farmers Co-operative Market in Du Bois, Pennsylvania. Jack Delano, photographer, 1940. P&P,FSA/OWI,LC-USF34-041314-D.

10-063. Boarding buses on a rainy market day, Lancaster, Pennsylvania. Marjory Collins, photographer, 1942. P&P,FSA/OWI,LC-USW3-010972-E.

10-063

BIBLIOGRAPHY

GENERAL WORKS

Kostof, Spiro. *The City Assembled: The Elements of Urban Form through History.* 1992. Reprint, New York: W. W. Norton, 2005.

———. *The City Shaped: Urban Patterns and Meanings through History.* Boston: Little, Brown, 1991.

Weiss, Walter M. *The Bazaar: Markets and Merchants of the Islamic World.* London: Thames and Hudson, 1998.

ENGINEERING, DESIGN, AND CONSTRUCTION

Di Macco, Sergio. *L'architettura dei mercati: Tecniche dell'edilizia annonaria* [The Architecture of Markets: Techniques for Building for Provisions]. Rome: Edizioni Kappa, 1993.

Friedmann, Alexandre. *Nouvelles Dispositions pour la Construction de Halles, Marchés et Entrepôts.* Paris: J. Boudry, 1877.

Gomes, Geraldo. "Artistic Intentions in Iron Architecture." *Journal of Decorative and Propaganda Arts, 1875–1945* 21 (1995): 87–106.

Moore, Richard Vincent. *L'architettura del mercato coperto: Dal Mercato all' Ipermercato* [The Architecture of the Covered Market: From the Market to the Supermarket]. Rome: Officina Edizioni, 1997.

Onderdonk, Francis S. *The Ferro-Concrete Style.* 1928. Reprint, Santa Monica: Hennessey & Ingalls, 1998.

Osthoff, Georg, and Eduard Schmitt. "Markthallen und Marktplätze." In *Handbuch der Architektur*, edited by Josef Durm, vol. 4, pt. 3: 2, 194–273. Darmstadt: Arnold Bergsträsser, 1891.

Pevsner, Nikolaus. *A History of Building Types.* Bollingen Series. Princeton: Princeton University Press, 1976.

Steiner, Frances H. *French Iron Architecture.* Ann Arbor, MI: UMI Research Press, 1984.

Taylor, Jeremy. "Charles Fowler: Master of Markets." *Architectural Review* 135 (1964): 174–82.

MARKETS IN EUROPE

Bailly, Gilles-Henri, and Philippe Laurent. *La France des Halles & Marchés.* Toulouse: Éditions Privat, 1998.

Barosso, Luisa, et al. *Mercati Coperti à Torino: Progetti, realizzazioni e tecnologie ottocentesche.* [Covered Markets in Turin: Nineteenth-Century Designs, Buildings, and Engineering]. Turin: Celid, 2000.

Cadilhon, Jean-Joseph, et al. "Wholesale Markets and Food Distribution in Europe: New Strategies for Old Functions." Center for Food Chain Research, Department of Agricultural Sciences, Imperial College, London. Discussion Paper No. 2, January 2003.

Calabi, Donatella, ed. *Fabbriche, Piazze, Mercati: La Città Italiana nel Rinascimento* [Buildings, Squares, Markets: The Italian City in the Renaissance]. Rome: Officina Edizioni, 1997.

———. *The Market and the City: Square, Street and Architecture in Early Modern Europe.* 1993. English ed. Burlington, VT: Ashgate, 2002.

Carson, John M. *Municipal Markets and*

Slaughterhouses in Europe. Department of Commerce and Labor, Bureau of Manufactures. Special Consular Reports, vol. 42, pt. 3. Washington, DC: Government Printing Office, 1910.

Città di Bra. *Le "agli" del mercato in provincial di Cuneo* [Market Halls in the Province of Cuneo]. Bra: Ministero Beni Culturali e Ambientali, Soprintendenza per I Beni Ambientali e Architettonici del Piemonte, Politecnico di Torino, 1992.

De la Pradelle, Michèle. *Market Day in Provence*. Translated by Amy Jacobs. Chicago: University of Chicago Press, 2006.

De Ligt, L. *Fairs and Markets in the Roman Empire: Economic and Social Aspects of Periodic Trade in a Pre-Industrial Society*. Dutch Monographs on Ancient History and Archaeology, vol. 11. Amsterdam: J. C. Geiben, 1993.

De Moncan, Patrice. *Baltard, Les Halles de Paris*. Paris: Les Éditions du Mécène, 1994.

Fitzpatrick, Anne Lincoln. *The Great Russian Fair: Nizhnii Novgorod, 1840–90*. New York: St. Martin's Press, 1990.

Frayn, Joan M. *Markets and Fairs in Roman Italy: Their Social and Economic Importance from the Second Century B.C. to the Third Century A.D.* Oxford: Clarendon Press, 1993.

Lemoine, Bertrand. *Les Halles de Paris*. Paris: L'Equerre, 1980.

Lohmeier, Andrew. "'Bürgerliche Gesellschaft' and Consumer Interests: The Berlin Public Market Hall Reform, 1867–1891," *Business History Review* 73 (Spring 1999): 91–113.

Masters, Betty R. *The Public Markets of the City of London Surveyed by William Leybourn in 1677*. London: London Topographical Society Publication No. 117, 1974.

Modigliani, Anna. *Mercati, Botteghe e Spazi di Commercio a Roma tra Medioevo ed Età Moderna* [Markets, Shops and Commercial Spaces in Rome from the Medieval to the Modern Era]. Rome: Roma nel Rinascimento, 1997.

Morrison, Kathryn A. *English Shops and Shopping*. New Haven and London: Yale University Press, 2003.

Newlands, James. *A Short Description of the Markets and Market Systems of Paris: With Notes on the Markets of London*. Liverpool: George M'Corquodale, 1865.

Obiols, Isabel, and Pere Ferrer. *The Boqueria Market: The Most Typical Market of Catalonia*. English ed. Barcelona: Salsa Books, 2004.

Pinon, Pierre. *Louis-Pierre et Victor Baltard*. Paris: Monum, Éditions du Patrimoine, 2005.

Risch, Theodor. *Bericht über Markthallen in Deutschland, Belgien, Frankreich, England und Italien* [Report on the Market Halls of Germany, Belgium, France, England, and Italy]. Berlin: Wolf Peiser, 1867.

Schmiechen, James, and Kenneth Carls. *The British Market Hall: A Social and Architectural History*. New Haven and London: Yale University Press, 1999.

Scola, Roger. *Feeding the Victorian City: The Food Supply of Manchester, 1770–1870*. Manchester and New York: Manchester University Press, 1992.

Siegel, Allan, ed. *Vásárcsarnok. The Market Hall. Expiration date: to be determined* [sic]. Budapest: Ernst Múzeum, 2005.

Thorne, Robert. *Covent Garden Market: Its History and Restoration*. London: Architectural Press, 1980.

MARKETS IN THE UNITED STATES

Cady, John Hutchins. "The Providence Market House and Its Neighborhood." *Rhode Island History* 11 (October 1952): 97–116.

Cooper, Constance J. *To Market, To Market, in Wilmington: King Street and Beyond*. Wilmington, DE: Cedar Tree Press, 1992.

Crow, William C. *The Wholesale Fruit and Vegetable Markets of New York City*. United States Department of Agriculture. Special Report. Washington, DC: Government Printing Office, 1940.

———. *Wholesale Markets for Fruits and Vegetables in 40 Cities*. United States Department of Agriculture. Circular 463. Washington, DC: Government Printing

Office, 1938.

De Voe, Thomas F. *The Market Book: A History of the Public Markets of the City of New York.* 1862. Reprint, New York: Augustus M. Kelley, 1970.

Goodwin, Arthur E. *Markets: Public and Private.* Seattle, WA: Montgomery Printing, 1929.

Goss, Jon. "Disquiet on the Waterfront: Reflections on Nostalgia and Utopia in the Urban Archetypes of Festival Marketplaces." *Urban Geography* 17, no. 3 (April 1996): 221–47.

Green, Bryan Clark. "The Structure of Civic Exchange: Market Houses in Early Virginia." In *Shaping Communities: Perspectives in Vernacular Architecture, VI,* edited by Carter L. Hudgins and Elizabeth Collins Cromley, 189–203. Knoxville: University of Knoxville Press, 1997.

Hild, Theodore. "The Galena Market House." *Material Culture* 32 (Fall 2000): 1–26.

King, Clyde Lyndon. *Public Markets in the United States.* Philadelphia: National Municipal League, 1917.

King, Clyde Lyndon, ed. *Reducing the Cost of Food Distribution.* Annals of the American Academy of Political and Social Science, vol. 50. Philadelphia: The Academy, 1913.

Larson, Olaf F., and Julie N. Zimmerman. *Sociology in Government: The Galpin-Taylor Years in the U.S. Department of Agriculture, 1919–1953.* University Park: Penn State Press, 2003.

Longstreth, Richard. *The Drive-In, the Supermarket, and the Transformation of Commercial Space in Los Angeles, 1914–1941.* Cambridge, MA: MIT Press, 1999.

Magoon, Charles E. *Photos at the Archives: A Descriptive Listing of 800 Historic Photographs on Food Marketing at the National Archives.* Santa Barbara, CA: McNally & Loftin, West, 1981.

———. *The Way It Was—The Produce Industry in the Early Years, 1890 to 1930: An Illustrated History.* Berkeley Springs, WV: 1997.

Mayo, James M. *The American Grocery Store: The Business Evolution of an Architectural Space.* Westport, CT: Greenwood Press, 1993.

———. "The American Public Market." *Journal of Architectural Education* 45 (November 1991): 41–57.

McCleary, Ann. "Negotiating the Urban Marketplace: Farm Women's Curb Markets in the 1930s." *Perspectives in Vernacular Architecture* 13 no. 1 (2006): 86–105.

New York City, Mayor's Market Commission. *Report of the Mayor's Market Commission of New York City,* December 1913.

Noonan Guerra, Mary Ann. *The History of San Antonio's Market Square.* San Antonio, TX: Alamo Press, 1988.

O'Neil, David K. *An Illustrated History of Reading Terminal Market.* Philadelphia: Camino Books, 2004.

Quincy, John, Jr. *Quincy's Market: A Boston Landmark.* Boston: Northeastern University Press, 2003.

Sauder, Robert A. "Municipal Markets in New Orleans," *Journal of Cultural Geography* 2 (Fall/Winter 1981): 82–95.

———. "The Origin and Spread of the Public Market System in New Orleans." *Louisiana History* 22 (Summer 1981): 281–97.

Shockley, Jay, et al. *Gansevoort Market Historic District: Designation Report.* New York: New York City Landmarks Preservation Commission, 2003.

Shorett, Alice, and Murray Morgan. *The Pike Place Market: People, Politics, and Produce.* Seattle, WA: Pacific Search Press, 1982.

Spitzer, Theodore, and Hilary Baum. *Public Markets and Community Revitalization.* Washington, DC: Urban Land Institute and Project for Public Spaces, 1995.

Tangires, Helen. "Adolf Cluss and Public Market Reform." In *Adolf Cluss, Architect: From Germany to America,* edited by Christof Mauch and Alan Lessoff. Washington, DC: German Historical Institute, 2005.

———. "Contested Space: The Life and Death of Center Market." *Washington History* 7 (Spring/Summer 1995): 46–67.

———. "The Country Connection: Farmers Markets in the Public Eye." *Pennsylvania Heritage* 24, no. 4 (Fall 1998): 4–11.

———. "Feeding the Cities: Public Markets

& Municipal Reform in the Progressive Era." *Prologue: Quarterly of the National Archives and Records Administration* 29 (Spring 1997): 16–26.

———. *Public Markets and Civic Culture in Nineteenth Century America*. Baltimore and London: Johns Hopkins University Press, 2003.

U.S. Department of Commerce. Bureau of the Census. *Municipal Markets in Cities Having a Population of over 30,000*. Washington, DC: Government Printing Office, 1919.

MARKETS IN CANADA

Biesenthal, Linda. *To Market, To Market: The Public Market Tradition in Canada*. Toronto: Peter Martin Associates, 1980.

MARKETS IN ASIA

Bestor, Theodor C. *Tsukiji: The Fish Market at the Center of the World*. Berkeley: University of California Press, 2004.

Hines, Thomas S. "American Modernism in the Philippines: The Forgotten Architecture of William E. Parsons." *Journal of the Society of Architectural Historians* 32, no. 4 (December 1973): 316–26.

STREET VENDORS

Beall, Karen. *Kaufrufe und Strassenhändler: Cries and Itinerant Trades*. Hamburg: Hauswedell, 1975.

Bluestone, Daniel M. " 'The Pushcart Evil': Peddlers, Merchants, and New York City's Streets, 1890–1940." *Journal of Urban History* 18 (November 1991): 68–92.

Burnstein, Daniel. "The Vegetable Man Cometh: Political and Moral Choices in Pushcart Policy in Progressive Era New York City." *New York History* (January 1996): 47–84.

Freeman, Roland L. *The Arabbers of Baltimore*. Centreville, MD: Tidewater Publishers, 1989.

Shesgreen, Sean. "The Cries of London in the Seventeenth Century." *Papers of the Bibliographical Society of America* 86 (1992): 269–94.

GLOSSARY

AGORA. Marketplace in ancient Greece.

AUCTION. A public sale in which property or items of merchandise are sold to the highest bidder.

BAZAAR. An oriental market or commercial district consisting of streets lined with shops and stalls (see also *souq*).

CENTRAL MARKET. A large retail and wholesale market that covers several city blocks under one roof or a series of roofs.

COMMISSION MERCHANT. An agent stationed at a market for the purpose of receiving goods from shippers and disposing of goods at a stipulated rate of commission on the selling price.

COOPERATIVE. A jointly owned commercial enterprise (usually organized by farmers or consumers) that produces and distributes goods and services and is run for the benefit of its owners.

CURB MARKET. Market conducted along a designated curb, section of a broad street, or vacant lot, where farmers sell to customers directly from their wagons or trucks, or from baskets and sacks on the curb.

FAIR. A gathering of buyers and sellers at a particular place and time for trade.

FARM WOMEN'S MARKET. Type of retail market established in the United States during the Great Depression for the purpose of promoting direct marketing of local produce, particularly fruits, vegetables, dairy products, eggs, and poultry, as well as cooked foods, handicrafts, flowers, and nursery stock.

FARMERS' MARKET. Market restricted to direct dealing between producer and consumer.

FESTIVAL MARKETPLACE. Themed specialty retail centers typically located on historic urban waterfronts (for example, Faneuil Hall Marketplace, Boston; Harborplace, Baltimore; South Street Seaport, New York).

FORUM. Marketplace in ancient Rome.

HUCKSTER. One who sells wares or provisions in the street; a peddler or hawker.

LOGGIA. A roofed arcade or gallery with open sides stretching along the front or side of a building.

MARKET ADJUNCT. A business, usually operated as a concession, that caters to the trade at markets (for example, restaurant; cold storage plant; slaughterhouse, grading, packing, and shipping service; cannery; supply store).

MARKET HOUSE. A building that functions primarily as a market for food.

MIDDLEMAN. Trader who buys from producers and sells to retailers or consumers; an intermediary or go-between.

PUSHCART. Wheeled vehicle that can be pushed by a person.

RETAILER. One who buys goods in large quantities from the producer either directly or through a wholesaler, and then sells individual items or small quantities to the general public or end-user customer.

SOUK (*souq, or suq*). Market or marketplace in the Islamic world (see also *bazaar*).

WHOLESALE MARKET. Market that exists for the convenience of producers of farm produce who wish to sell in large quantities, and for the convenience of grocers, hucksters, hotels, restaurants, and other purchasers who wish to buy in large quantities.

WHOLESALE TERMINAL MARKET. Market complex dedicated to the large-scale storage and regional distribution of food by means of coordinated rail, water, and road ways.

WHOLESALER. One who buys goods in large quantities from their producers, manufacturers, or importers and then sells smaller quantities to retailers, who in turn sell to the general public.

INDEX

Locators that include a section designator followed by a hyphen (e.g., IN-010, 3-090, 2-153) refer to numbered captions. All other locators are page numbers. Individuals who created the original images used in this collection, or the structures depicted, are identified as follows: ph. = photographer; del. = delineator; eng. = engraver; ill. = illustrator; bldr. = builder; arch. = architect; art. = artist; engr = engineer.

ABOUT THE CD-ROM

The CD-ROM includes direct links to four of the most useful online catalogs and sites, which you may choose to consult in locating and downloading images included on it or related items. Searching directions, help, and search examples (by text or keywords, titles, authors or creators, subject or location, and catalog and reproduction numbers, etc.) are provided online, in addition to information on rights and restrictions, how to order reproductions, and how to consult the materials in person.

1. The Prints & Photographs Online Catalog (PPOC) (http://www.loc.gov/rr/print/catalogabt.html) contains over one million catalog records and digital images representing a rich cross-section of graphic documents held by the Prints & Photographs Division and other units of the Library. It includes a majority of the images on this CD-ROM and many related images, such as those in the HABS and HAER collections cited below. At this writing the catalog provides access through group or item records to about 50 percent of the Division's holdings.

SCOPE OF THE PRINTS AND PHOTOGRAPHS ONLINE CATALOG

Although the catalog is added to on a regular basis, it is not a complete listing of the holdings of the Prints & Photographs Division, and does not include all the items on this CD-ROM. It also overlaps with some other Library of Congress search systems. Some of the records in the PPOC are also found in the LC Online Catalog, mentioned below, but the P&P Online Catalog includes additional records, direct display of digital images, and links to rights, ordering, and background information about the collections represented in the catalog. In many cases, only "thumbnail" images (GIF images) will display to those searching outside the Library of Congress because of potential rights considerations, while onsite searchers have access to larger JPEG and TIFF images as well. There are no digital images for some collections, such as the Look Magazine Photograph Collection. In some collections, only a portion of the images have been digitized so far. For further information about the scope of the Prints & Photographs online catalog and how to use it, consult the Prints & Photographs Online Catalog *HELP* document.

WHAT TO DO WHEN DESIRED IMAGES ARE NOT FOUND IN THE CATALOG

For further information about how to search for Prints & Photographs Division holdings not represented in the online catalog or in the lists of selected images, submit an email using the "Ask a Librarian" link on the Prints & Photographs Reading Room home page or contact: Prints & Photographs Reading Room, Library of Congress, 101 Independence Ave., SE, Washington, D.C. 20540-4730 (telephone: 202-707-6394).

2. The American Memory site (http://memory.loc.gov), a gateway to rich primary source materials relating to the history and culture of the United States. The site offers more than seven million digital items from more than 100 historical collections.

3. The Library of Congress Online Catalog (http://catalog.loc.gov/) contains approximately 13.6 million records representing books, serials, computer files, manuscripts, cartographic materials, music, sound recordings, and visual materials. It is especially useful for finding items identified as being from the Manuscript Division and the Geography and Map Division of the Library of Congress.

4. Built in America: Historic American Buildings Survey/Historic American Engineering Record, 1933–Present (http://memory.loc.gov/ammem/collections/habs_haer) describes and links to the catalog of the Historic American Buildings Survey (HABS) and the Historic American Engineering Record (HAER), among the most heavily represented collections on the CD-ROM.